Celebrating Who We Are

Celebrating Who We Are

Edited transcripts of Headless Way workshops

RICHARD LANG

The Shollond Trust
London

Published by The Shollond Trust
87B Cazenove Road, London N16 6BB, England
www.headless.org
headexchange@gn.apc.org

The Shollond Trust is a UK charitable trust, reg. no. 1059551

ISBN 978-1-908774-26-2

Illustrations by Victor Lunn-Rockliffe
Cover design by rangsgraphics.com
Interior design by Richard Lang

for Joy and Dale

Contents

Introduction

Between 2011 and 2015 Dale Shimizu recorded ten of my workshops. Early in 2016 Dale sent me the audio files, suggesting there were many questions, responses and interactions which could be of value to people interested in seeing who they really are. I began listening and realised he was right. So I transcribed and edited the recordings, combining them into the shape of one workshop—this book.

As you read you will be guided through the Headless Way experiments—they point directly to your True Self. Hopefully you will feel you are participating in a workshop, exploring with others the experience and meaning of who you really are. You will see how different people react to this neutral, non-verbal experience in a variety of ways—from one end of the spectrum to the other!

As well as guiding our attention to our True Self, a workshop keeps the experience on the front burner. If you want to stay awake to who you really are, there's nothing quite like spending time with others who are also Seeing. It is highly infectious. I hope this book infects you!

The Headless Way was developed by the British philosopher Douglas Harding (1909–2007). Soon after meeting Douglas in 1970 (I was 17) I knew I wanted to help share Seeing with the world. Though I didn't have much experience of other spiritual paths, I could see that the Headless Way was astonishingly direct and effective. It was special, a new development, a breakthrough in terms of making quickly and easily available the experience of our True Self. Douglas made many friends who appreciated the simplicity and effectiveness of his 'experiments', a loose-knit community of friends where Seeing was natural and normal. Gradually, as Seeing becomes more widely known, so this community grows. If you want friends who value their True Self, they are there. It is up to you to make contact.

Looking back on Douglas Harding's work I see that the way in which he communicated Seeing evolved over the years—for example, the development of the experiments in the late '60s and early '70s was a major change in his style of presentation. As I continue the work of pointing to our True Self using the experiments, I see that my own style also evolves. For instance, I used to think, naively, that being aware of my True Self would mean the dissolving of my sense of separateness—the source of so much if not all of my suffering. But I have come to see that not only does this feeling of being separate not go away, it is in fact a great blessing. This deeper awareness of the value of both sides of our identity, the self as well as the Self, is reflected in this book.

Over the last few years I have also become more aware of the importance and power of communicating this Reality to others. As you will see, in a workshop I invite participants to communicate their experience of their True Self to each other. This acknowledgement of our Common Identity is a beautiful, profoundly respectful and loving thing to do. In fact I can't think of any greater respect I could give to another person than acknowledging who they really are.

In his great book *The Hierarchy of Heaven & Earth*, Douglas Harding suggested, with characteristic understatement, that the map of our place in the universe presented in that book was but a sketch, and he invited others to fill out that sketch with detailed research. That book is so full of wonderful detail that when I first read it I wondered what he meant by further research. But in his later books Harding did some of that research—looking into how Seeing works out in different areas of life. For example, his article *The Face Game* (and his book by that name) explores the contribution that Seeing makes to Transactional Analysis. As you will discover in this book, I have in my own way continued exploring the implications of Seeing, in particular Harding's idea of four main stages of personal development—the baby, the child, the adult and the seer.

But I've said enough by way of introduction. Now I want to invite you to join the workshop. Jump in. Treat yourself to an adventure!

Richard Lang

Chapter 1
Straight to the Experience

Richard: It's at this point I realise I haven't thought about this workshop at all!

Sarah: Nice. You are going to be surprised too.

Richard: Yes, I am! Alright, this workshop is about who we really are—about seeing who we really are and a bit about understanding who we really are, but the understanding is going to be different for each of us.

Probably most of you have heard about your True Self in some form or other. This workshop is a modern approach to the question 'Who am I?' You are going to take a fresh look at yourself. You are going to look at the one sitting on your chair—from your point of view. You have all the information you need for this investigation because the subject of the investigation is on your chair!

I'd like you to notice something very simple and obvious about yourself—you can't see your own face. Can anyone see their own face? I can't. There's one face I do not see in this group and it's Richard's. There's one face you can't see in this group and it's yours.

We start visually—noticing you can't see your face. We are bringing our attention to this simple fact. This is so simple you can't get it wrong. The whole day is about bringing our attention to this perspective—to what we are from our own point of view. Today I am here as a friend to share with you this experience of who we are and to explore our different reactions to it.

Hold your hands out in front of you like this. You see your hands and the room beyond.

Bring your hands slowly towards you. Your hands get bigger.

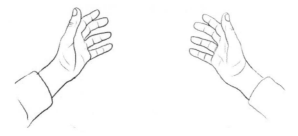

Move them past either side of your head. Your fingers disappear, then your hands disappear, all the way to your wrists.

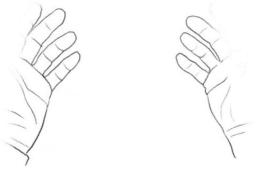

Now bring your hands forward so you can see them again. They come out of 'nothing'. I call this the Great Void, the Emptiness in which everything is happening, the Silence in which all sounds are arising. You can call it what you like. Most of the time it means the world to me, although sometimes it doesn't mean anything at all! Today isn't about taking on board a particular meaning, it's about exploring our unique reactions to this experience. You can't get it wrong. You can't get either the experience or your reaction wrong.

Let's do that again. This is meditation. It's not something you learn. It's not something you see once and then just think about or remember, it's something you keep paying attention to. You keep looking for yourself. This is attending to your view of you, the First Person view. Your view of you is going to be different from what everybody else sees of you.

Move your hands past either side of your head again. Your hands get huge and then, without any pain, dissolve into nothing. You are guiding your attention to the place you are looking out of. You are looking as if for the first time at this secret place. How clear and empty and spacious it is. How still and quiet. Now bring your hands forward—magically they emerge out of Nothing, out of this mysterious Awareness. This is the most obvious thing in the world. You couldn't get more obvious than this.

Dale: The first time I did that experiment, perhaps ten years ago—I think it was in Douglas' book that I first heard about it—it was an immediate shift. I felt I had put on Awareness. All of a sudden it brought that from the background to the foreground. Undeniable.

Richard: Yes. Putting on clear, boundless Awareness. Hold your hands out in front of you again and look at the space between your hands. It's a small space. As you bring your hands towards you the space between your hands gets wider and wider until you get to the moment just before you dissolve your hands into the Emptiness. The space between your hands is now as wide as the room. Is that true? Yes. And when you put your hands right into the Emptiness, then the boundary goes and the Space goes on for ever. Infinitely wide.

This is a non-verbal experience. It doesn't have to mean anything. It's also a non-emotional experience. It's not about feeling good or bad. You will have a different reaction to this experience from me. Brilliant! There isn't a right reaction, a right thought or understanding or feeling. It's a neutral experience. On the one hand that doesn't sound very attractive, but on the other hand, as I think we may discover, it is one of its great strengths. It is not dependent on what you feel.

You don't have to believe anything I say. You are the authority on you. We have to use words to communicate but the words are not the thing. I might call this the Void, the Great Space, Emptiness, the True Self, the Openness here, this Clarity, Stillness, the place I am looking out of, my No-face, my No-head... Because we have got the experience, because you can't get it wrong, we are free to use different words—we don't need to get stuck on any one way of describing it.

How long does it take you to notice you cannot see your face? How quick can you get Home? Have you seen the adverts for cars that tell you how fast they can accelerate from 0 to 60 mph? Of course, the faster the better. The Headless Way is like a fast car! It's a fast-track spiritual Way. Put your hands into the Void. That didn't take long, did it? The experiments are a breakthrough. The Headless Way is unique—it has experiments that other spiritual paths do not use. We charge a lot to use them—all the experiments are patented. I'm joking!

We start visually but we will also look into this in the context of the other senses, how it relates to thoughts and feelings, how it works out in our lives, how to keep this going and that kind of thing. We've got the whole day. We will stay with the visual experiments a bit longer—it's a good place to start because it's easy to communicate who we really are using vision.

Right from the beginning you can be aware of something that comes with this observation—because you don't see your face, what do you see instead?

David: All the faces around you.

Richard: Yes. We call it 'trading faces'. You've got Richard's face now and I've got yours. Whenever you look at anyone you take on their face and give them your own. Without effort. Without even having to understand anything. It's just the way it is. You are built Open for others. Wide-open, clear, in a completely safe way. This is non-verbal and obvious. You don't need to understand anything to see it, do you? No. You don't have to feel anything in particular to see it. It's incredible. It's brilliant.

Dale: What I appreciate the most in this particular approach is the immediacy of the recognition. To start the journey from that place of No-place is essential because the confusion that comes with being identified as a seeker and all that is completely dispelled right from the immediacy of seeing this for oneself. The non-verbal pointing is wonderful. Then the deconstructive enquiry and everything else that you hear afterwards makes sense. But when you don't have the direct experience, that stuff stays out there as just thought. It doesn't penetrate to the core.

Richard: Thank you. We're going to have an ongoing conversation about this all day. We're going to do lots of experiential things and I hope you feel welcome to share your reactions as we go along because it's inspiring for everyone to hear different people's reactions. The One likes to hear itself speaking with many voices! There will be lots of opportunities to share as we go through the day. As I say, everyone will have a different reaction. I welcome that. We are not here to agree. Let's get that out of the way!

Anne: I like that.

Richard: Especially with me — don't agree with me! What we are primarily here to do is to attend to what it's like to be oneself. You can't get that wrong. You are in the perfect location to see what you are at Centre. This approach is experimental, it is modern, it is simple and direct. And the best way of hanging out with this during this workshop is to be open-minded. Relax as much as you can and be open-minded and curious.

As I've said, I will be encouraging you to use your voices today, to affirm your observation of who you really are in public. Awareness of who we really are grows when we bring it onto the front burner and articulate it. Do you see your own face right now?

Michael: No!

Richard: Do you see everyone else's instead?

Michael: Yes!

Richard: I'm not asking you to say anything that isn't true. If it's not true for you, don't say it. Obviously others can see your face and you can see it in the mirror, and you can imagine it, but you can't see it at your Centre. I can't see mine here at my Centre. This is obvious stuff, isn't it? Incredibly obvious. We're not starting with a difficult, mystical theory. We are doing something a five-year-old could do.

Obviously you can see your nose. If you close one eye your nose is rather large—in fact you've got the largest nose in the room! It goes from the ceiling to the floor. But it isn't attached to anything. It emerges out of nothing.

If anyone at this point is thinking, 'Oh my God, what on earth have I come to today?'—it's very simple. We are observing what it's like to be oneself. We are noticing the difference between our public identity which is what we look like *to others*, and our private identity which is what we are *for ourselves*. Only you can see what you are for yourself. It's a secret thing. One reason I might under-value my True Self is because no one else can see it. I think I must be wrong and everyone else must be right because I'm the only one that can see my facelessness. Everyone else tells me I have a face here. There are twenty of you in this room and one of me so I'm outnumbered. I get talked out of the reality of my facelessness. But now I'm putting the record straight. You are right from there, I do have a face for you—and I am right from here, I don't have one for me. This difference between your private and your public identity is incredible. Looking out from my No-face I take on your faces, I take on the world—I'm Space for the whole world!

Let me make clear from the beginning that seeing who you really are is not necessarily a 'wow' experience. It's simply being attentive to what it's like to be you, whatever you are feeling. If you are not having a 'wow' experience it's okay, you are still seeing who you really are.

Joy: I am definitely missing something.

Richard: I don't think you are. Can you see your face?

Joy: No.

Richard: That's it. As I've said, we are distinguishing between that simple observation and how we react to it or what it means to us. You've got the experience but what it means to you will be different from what it means to me or Dale or anyone else. It might even mean nothing to you. So we distinguish between our reactions and the experience. The idea of the workshop is to approach this experience from different angles, not just visual but also non-visual, and hang out with it for the day and see what it means to us — if anything. But I assure you, you have got the experience because you cannot see your face. When you look at me now, whose face do you see?

Joy: Yours.

Richard: Yes. So we say we are 'face-to-No-face'. Is that true? Yes. So you have Richard's face now and not Joy's, yes? That's rather beautiful, isn't it?

Dale: I don't know if Joy remembers — one time I had a powerful experience of the face-to-No-face experience. I was looking in the mirror and suddenly I had the deep experience that there was no head here and there was a face there. It really settled in. Then I noticed the characteristics of that one in the mirror in a very detached way. Then I apologised to Joy saying, 'I'm sorry that you have to see that one because I don't!' I felt empathy for her! I get the better part of the trade!

Richard: Yes, like that limerick attributed to Woodrow Wilson –

As a beauty I'm not a star –
There are others more handsome by far –
But my face, I don't mind it,
For I am behind it:
It's those in front get the jar.

I'm going to place this experience of facelessness in various contexts. First, consider what the great spiritual traditions say. When you boil them down to their essence they are saying one thing, which is that right where you are is a miracle. This Miracle was not born and won't die. Everything comes and goes except this Miracle, the Miracle of Being—the Miracle of the One Self. The great mystics claim that you are that One Self, that Miracle—within you is the Kingdom of Heaven, God, the Alone. What an astonishing claim! Today in this workshop we are testing that claim. The great mystics say that most people are not aware of who they really are. They say it's incredible that people are not aware of it because it's so obvious—you must be drunk not to see it. But if you do see it, and if you live consciously from who you really are, it is life-changing. That's the promise. It is up to each of us to test that claim, that promise.

Chapter 2

Peeling the Onion

Richard: Here's a model of the self designed by Douglas Harding in the 1970s—the Youniverse Explorer. (Douglas Harding worked out the philosophy of the Headless Way and invented the experiments.) This model indicates that what you are depends on where someone is observing you from.

You are looking at me from several feet so you see a person here, but if you came up to me with the right instruments you would lose my human appearance and instead you would find a patch of skin and then cells. If you came up to my cells then you'd find molecules. It's like peeling an onion. If you came up to my molecules—I'm disappearing fast now!—you would find particles. You are moving in towards the Nothing at my Centre. You can get very close but you can never get right to me here at zero distance and see what I am here. But I am here and I see I am Nothing.

If you went away from me instead, eventually you'd see Levittown, then America, then the planet and the star. These are all appearances of me and of you. It's beautiful. They are layers of our body. We need every one of these layers to sit here and breathe. I need my lungs, I need the cells that make up my lungs and the molecules that make up my cells. I also need the atmosphere, the sunlight… It's one beautiful living system. It functions. This is who we are. Amazing. This is a new way of appreciating ourselves. We need to catch up with science, with what it is telling us about ourselves.

Not only does science reflect back this many-levelled body of ours, we identify with many of these layers. I identify with being Richard, with being English, European, with being planetary—hopefully I identify with my planet sometimes. Then I expand to feel for my star. If we were being attacked by another star—if Star Wars broke out—our star would be under threat. I would feel in danger. Then the next moment I might be identifying with my football team—I contract. One moment I'm concerned with my solar system, the next moment I'm thinking about that goal we missed. Then it's my aching knee, then the state of the economy! All the time we are expanding and contracting.

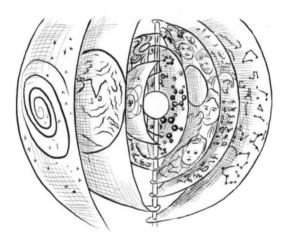

The pictures on the outsides of the layers of the model represent what others see you to be from various distances. The pictures on the insides represent your view out from your central Nothingness. When you look out only a little way then you see your nose and the rest of your headless body. Looking further you see other people. Looking even further you see buildings, clouds, then the Moon, the stars, the galaxies. The view out from your Empty Centre is layered like the view in. It's a beautiful set-up. So when I say I'm looking in at my Centre, I mean the Centre of all these layers. This model places the experience of your central Nothingness in the context of your beautiful many-levelled body-mind. We have not yet really woken up to our many-levelled body-mind. We know it piecemeal and think of ourselves as a tiny part of it, but now, looking at this model, we can understand it is one living organism.

The main question we are asking today is, 'Who or what is at the Centre of all these layers?' Others can tell you what your body looks like at these various ranges—your beautiful body—but no one can tell you what you are at the Centre of all these layers except you because only you are there. The transparent sphere at the centre of the model represents you at zero distance. The purpose of our experiments is to direct our attention to the Centre of all our layers—to observe the Reality behind all our appearances. The world's great mystics say that at Centre you are the One, the Source, God. When I look here at zero distance I don't find my face or anything—I find this Openness which is full of the many-levelled universe. I now verify that the mystics got it right!

Move your hands back to the place you are looking out of. Here you are Empty and Clear. Here you are self-evidently aware, awake. Here you can say, 'Yes, I AM.'

Dale: When Richard introduced this, this model really helped me to connect a lot of things I was exploring. Obviously the spiritual question is, 'Who or what is truly here?' To begin with I wasn't on a spiritual path and this, my appearance, was the only reality for me. And that's all I could see of you. You are this too. I knew about the other dimensions—the closer I got the more I began to disappear. But I still didn't know this Centre, at that point. I notice a lot of people become preoccupied with one of these dimensions more than the others. Biologist seem to get more preoccupied with this cellular layer, a psychologist is more preoccupied with this human one, an ecologist with another one. Everyone has a piece of the pie. But no one was questioning this one at the Centre. This one was always overlooked by me because it's not like any of these in the sense that it never comes and goes, it has no shape, no colour. How do we draw attention to this Reality? This is why we do the experiments. It's brilliant. I can't see what is here. It is very simple and yet none of these other layers ever occur outside of this Space. I have never had one of these experiences outside of this Capacity. This model is brilliant, the way it brings everything together. You could contemplate this endlessly.

Chapter 3

The Pointing Experiment

Richard: Here is a simple experiment for testing what the great spiritual teachers say about who we all really are at Centre, to see if what they say is true. We are going to point at ourselves and look and see what we are. How simple is that! First we will direct our attention to things that are distant, then to things that are closer, then right to the place we are looking out of.

For this exercise you need a finger. Everyone got a finger? Did you bring it? I don't know if we put that on the list of things to bring!

First point at the floor. The reason for pointing is to direct your attention. Look at what you are pointing at. You see the colours and shapes there. It's a thing. This is simple and obvious—you don't need to ask anyone else what's there, you look for yourself.

Now point at your shoe—it's also a thing. You don't have to understand how your shoe was made to see it, you just look. Point at your knee—it's also a thing.

Point at your torso. You see colours and shapes and perhaps the movement of your breath there.

Now hold your finger out in front of you and point back at where others see your face. What do you see where you are pointing?

You don't see your face, do you? No. You are pointing at a very special place, the place you are looking out of.

You don't need to ask anyone else what is there because you can look for yourself. In fact no one else has the authority to tell you what is there because they are all several feet away whilst only you are there. You are the only one your side of your finger. Everyone else will say you are pointing at your face — that's what they see from a distance. But you are your side of your finger, at zero distance. What do you find there? I find no face here — no colours here, no shapes, no movement, no boundary, no age — nothing.

You are being your own authority on what it's like right where you are, the place you are looking out of, the place you are living from. Are you small there or are you boundless? I am boundless, still, silent.

Do you have to have a name for this to see it? No. Do you have to understand how it was made? No.

This is a non-verbal experience. You can describe it as you like — because we've got the experience we can use whichever words are meaningful to us. Now, three or four of you, how would you describe this?

Participants: Nothing. Frustrating. Like a reflection. A window. Transparency. Expanse. Mystery.

Two-way pointing
Now use the index finger on your other hand to point out at the same time.

16

That finger is pointing into the room. It's pointing at a thousand colours and shapes and movement and so on. This indicates that this Space that you are at Centre isn't just empty, it's also full. True? Yes. It's a full Space. It's empty-for-filling. Right now it's full of this room and all the people in it. It's also full of sounds and feelings and thoughts. In that outward direction it is full of life and colour and everything.

This two-way pointing gesture also indicates there's no dividing line between the Space and what's in the Space. I can't see my No-head without seeing what is happening in it. I can't see the Void without seeing the forms that are arising in it. Here at Centre it is simple and empty, there it's complicated, full of things — and these two different aspects are not separate.

Today, in a number of different ways, we will be bringing our attention back to our True Self, this Open Space, this Awareness that is always full of something. The joy of spending the day together is that this Awareness is on the front burner all day. It's the easiest thing to see it, but to keep seeing it, to stay aware of it — that is what we are doing today. As well as pointing to this Reality, this workshop is about resting in it and celebrating it and sharing our different reactions to it. Any reflections to share at the moment?

Paul: When we point and we look, does everyone see the same thing?

Richard: When you point there do you see any colour there?

Paul: No.

Richard: I don't see a shape here. Do you see one there?

Paul: No.

Richard: So it's the same in those respects, right?

Paul: Correct.

Richard: I don't see any movement here. Do you see any movement there?

Paul: No.

Richard: It seems like we are agreeing.

Paul: We are.

Richard: My seeing in the outward direction stops at whatever I am looking at, but when I look back it doesn't stop anywhere. Is that true for you?

Paul: Sure.

Richard: It's looking like it's the same here for me as it is for you there. This two-way pointing gesture indicates two directions, in and out. The view out from each of us is different but the view in is the same because it is nothing. It has no shape, no colour, no movement...

Bill: I found it disconcerting when we did the experiment—the first time you realise you are the only 'you'. You are surrounded by people but still I am the person that is me, I am the one that interprets for me. It's disconcerting.

Richard: Is it the feeling of being alone?

Bill: Yes, exactly.

Richard: When we think of ourselves as being alone, in a crowd say, we might feel lonely. We feel separate from others. But when you see this, this Aloneness is different because it includes others, doesn't it? It's not a separative thing. This Space now has everyone's face in it. This is 'aloneness by inclusion' which is a different thing from 'aloneness by exclusion'.

I think that if at any point you feel this experience is disconcerting, that's very good news. It means you are taking it seriously. You are nodding your head there...

Barbara: It's startling. You see the room and everyone so much more holistically than you did before. I walk in—it's been a frazzle this morning—and I sit down and there are all these people and then I see all these heads and this Space and it startles you awake.

Richard: Seeing this is being awake. And though it's startling and fresh it's familiar too, would you say?

Barbara: Yes.

Andrew: It's always been there. It never wasn't there. It's more than familiar! It's always there.

Brian: It's always there but it's so easy to get it all muddied up and lose sight of it.

Richard: Yes. We overlook it. We look the wrong way, in a way.

Brian: We should all walk backwards! If you walk backwards, it becomes forefront!

Richard: There's a two-faced Roman God called Janus. One of his faces is looking forwards and the other is looking backwards. You could say that's a metaphor for this, for two-way looking. You are looking in both directions at once — in to the Space and out to the world.

You've got the non-verbal experience. You can't get Nothing more than you've got it now. The experience is absolutely simple and the same for us all. You don't see your head, instead you see the world. Is that true for you?

Brian: Yes.

Richard: Yes! This is very important, to say in public what you experience — 'Yes, instead of my head I see the world here.' I think it's important to say this out loud because, one way or another, all day long we are affirming the opposite — that we are separate things. When I say, 'I am Richard', I am taking up your point of view of me. I am saying, 'I accept I am here what you see me to be from there.' But now I am saying, 'No! It's not like that here. For me I am not Richard, I am Space for the world!' I am speaking up for my own point of view.

I'm not trying to pull the wool over your eyes or convince you of anything that isn't true. You are the authority on what it is like to be you.

Diana: I can feel something here.

Richard: Alright, let's look at that. Be aware of the sensation of your forehead. Does that sensation have a colour?

Diana: No.

Richard: How wide is it?

Diana: I can't tell.

Richard: Do the sensations you feel there make a solid, coloured thing there, a head there, or are they just sensations in Awareness? My sensations are just sensations in Awareness. They don't make

19

a head here.

George: I can see my glasses.

Richard: Look at your glasses. You can see their oval shape. Whatever you can see of your glasses, there it is in your view out. But do you see your face behind your glasses?

George: No.

Richard: The Space on your side of your glasses is absolutely clear. Glasses bring the world into focus but they don't change the Space, and they don't obstruct your view of the Space. You are looking through your glasses from the Space.

George: I'm having the sensation that this Reality is like being at the movies.

Richard: Yes, and there's no one watching.

George: What you mean?

Richard: When we point here we point at our No-face. When you point out with your other hand you are pointing at everything in the room. This 'two-way pointing' indicates that this Emptiness here isn't just empty it's also full—of the movie. There's the movie. In the movie you can see the frame of your glasses—and your big nose! But your side of the movie it's empty. There isn't a person there watching it. Anything you experience is in the movie—your thoughts and feelings and reactions and sensations, including the sensation of your head. It's a multi-sense movie. But this side of all that is Space for all that.

Undoubtedly seeing this will bring up questions and difficulties and problems for many of us. You say, 'Yes, but…' Great! If it didn't bring up difficulties and problems it would be rather odd because this is a very different way of seeing yourself from the social view. The social view is what others see you to be—with a head, with a background behind you, separate from others. What we are doing today is taking seriously our own point of view.

Of course the important thing is how you apply this in your life. That really is the test. Does being awake to your True Nature actually make a difference in your life? I say it does. For example, when I look at you and notice I have your face instead of my own, I realise, 'Your face is mine. There's no distance. I am built Open for you. It's face there to No-face here. I am absolutely Empty for you. There's nothing here in your way.' This has deep implications for the way we relate to others. I look at Phil now and I say, 'You have got Richard's face instead of Phil's and I have got your face instead of mine.' We call it, 'trading faces'. 'You are in me, I am in you', is another way of putting it. This is a profound remedy for feeling separate, isolated, lonely. In fact, realising everyone is within you is love — seeing you are built Open for others, that you are others, is the basis of love.

This workshop is about helping each other keep this Awareness on the front burner. It's infectious. Today we are infecting each other with awareness of who we really are.

Chapter 4

The Single Eye

Richard: Here's another visual experiment. We will come to the non-visual in a moment.

Notice how many eyes you are looking out of. Why do I ask this? Because if you are looking out of two eyes then you are a 'thing' and you are separate from the rest of the world. You are enclosed within that solid thing there, your head—imprisoned in there. But what if you have made a mistake? What if you aren't imprisoned? What if you aren't cooped up inside a head there, peering out of two little windows but instead are wide-open, at large, free? It's worth taking a few minutes to see what you are looking out of—whether you are in prison or not! If you are making a fundamental mistake about what you are at Centre, then it's likely your mistake will be affecting how you relate to others, affecting how you live—it may well be messing up your whole life!

So let's take a fresh look at the place we are looking out of to see what we are. How many eyes are you looking out of in your own experience? To test this we hold our hands out like this and make two holes like a pair of glasses, or if you wear glasses you can hold them out in front of you instead.

There's a dividing line between the two holes or lenses, and in each hole or lens there's a different view. Slowly put them on as if you are putting on glasses. Watch what happens to the dividing line. Put them right on. What has happened to the dividing line?

Ellen: It's disappeared.

James: The two become one.

Richard: Yes. We call this the Single Eye. I see two eyes in the mirror, others see two eyes when they look at me and I can imagine two here—but I only see One here.

Bring your hands to the edge of the field of view—what I call 'the View'—and notice that all the way round it your hands disappear into this Opening, this Single Eye. One big Eye! Everything is inside that Eye. Are you looking out of a Single Eye?

Participants: Yes.

Richard: It's a powerful thing to admit in public the truth about who we really are. I confess to all of you that I have one Eye! I am looking out of one Opening, everyone is in my Single Eye! Of course it's not an 'eye'—it has no colour or shape. 'Eye' is a convenient name for it.

Natasha is a friend who lives in Moscow. She's attended several workshops so she's done this experiment. One day she was walking down the street and a little boy she didn't know stopped her and asked if he could show her a magic trick. Natasha agreed. He held up two pastries shaped like doughnuts and declared, 'I can make these two become one!' 'Okay, show me,' Natasha replied. You can guess what happened next—he put them on like we've just done with our hands. Of course Natasha knew what he was seeing. Then he asked her, 'Do you want to try?' So she put them on and of course she saw the two holes become one. But as he was watching her his jaw dropped with disappointment—'Oh, it doesn't work for you!' I guess he hadn't quite sorted out the difference between himself as he saw himself with One Eye and the way others saw him with two eyes. Perhaps this was a significant moment in his development, the moment he realised: 'No one can see my Single Eye except me!' It's not a very long way from there to saying, 'Since no one can see my Single Eye but me, I don't have a Single Eye. Everyone tells me I've got two eyes—they must be right and I must be wrong. So now I accept I've got two eyes.' That's stepping into the two-eyed box.

How big is the view?

Look at any two objects in the room. You can compare their sizes. You say this one's a bit wider than that one, and that's a bit taller than that one and so on. Anything in this room is either bigger, smaller or roughly the same size as something else. In this sense an object's size is relative.

Now be aware of the Whole View, your One Eye. How big is it?

Kevin: Never ending.

Richard: Never ending! There isn't a second one on the right or the left to compare it with, is there? You can't say yours is bigger than someone else's because you don't see anyone else's. There isn't another one to compare yours with. Your Eye is incomparable so you can't say how big it is. True? If you could see another one, then okay, you could compare yours with that one, but there isn't another one, is there? Have you ever seen another View apart from your own?

Ellen: I just got that!

Richard: Can anyone see another one? If so, where?

Dale: I wouldn't tell you!

Richard: You wouldn't tell me! You can only see one Eye — yours. Other people tell you about their Single Eyes but you have never seen them. In Tibetan Buddhism, in Dzogchen, they talk about 'the View'. What is 'the View'? The View is what you are looking at! It is your Single Eye. Because you are looking directly at the View you are in exactly the right place to see what it is. How big is the View? You don't have to look up its size in a book. You don't have to ask someone else. They might be wrong! You look for yourself. To see how big the View is, put your hands on either side of your face — on either side of your No-face — like horse-blinkers. You see everything is between your huge hands. Your Eye has the world inside it, right? It's big!

James: It's as big as the universe.

Richard: It is, isn't it! Wow!

James: Yes, wow!

Richard: This morning in our Facebook group someone posted a story from a classroom of young children. The children were asked, 'What is the biggest thing in the world?' One child said her dad, another said an elephant, but a third said, 'my eye.' The teacher asked her, 'Why your eye?' She replied, 'Because my eye contains her dad and the elephant and everything.' Isn't that amazing?

In the film Jurassic Park there's a big guy. He forgets that if you don't want to be seen by a raptor you must stay still because although a raptor's eyesight is not very good, it notices movement. But he moves! That was the end of him. Movement attracts attention. It's a primal thing. Bring your hands back to the edge of your Single Eye, to the edge of the View and move them around there. The movement of your hands attracts your attention right to the edge where they disappear. Move them in and out of the Space. I don't think you'll be able to describe that edge adequately in words, but you are experiencing it. Put aside your assumptions about what that edge is like and look as if for the first time, like a child.

Is the view inside anything?

Look at an object in front of you. Whatever object you are observing is right in the middle of your field of view. Towards the edge of the field of view things get vaguer and more blurry until you reach the region where you can't see anything. Someone last night called this region the 'event horizon'—where there's nothing more to see. All the way around the View you can't see anything—is that true?

Jennifer: Yes.

Richard: Look at any object in the room. It's got a boundary and there's something all the way around that boundary. Look at this piece of paper on the floor—there's floor all the way around it. It's within that bigger environment. Everything you look at is located inside an environment, it's surrounded by other things. I look at Mark—there's an edge around him. Inside that edge is Mark, outside him is the rest of the room. There isn't a part of Mark's edge where there's nothing beyond it. There are things all the way around him.

Now look at the Whole View, all the way to the event horizon. Can you see anything around it?

Jennifer: It's surrounded by what you can't see. By what you are not seeing.

Richard: Yes. I don't see anything there. Wow! It's not inside anything, is it? The Whole View is hanging there in Nothing. It doesn't have a hook on the top that attaches it to something above it.

Jennifer: There's no border or shape to it. There's no boundary, it disappears into nothing.

Richard: Amazing!

Jennifer: It disappears into this Void.

Richard: Into the Void. We can call this Void whatever we like—Consciousness, Awareness, the Great Spirit, the Land of Everlasting Clearness, Silence, Stillness.

Jennifer: It has no limits.

Richard: You said it in public! It has no limits. It's not inside an environment! It's hanging in Nothing. The Whole View is suspended in Nothing. Every individual thing is within this View but the Whole View itself is within Nothing, projected on Nothing, happening in Nothing! It's not inside anything. It's free. Free and stress-free—there's nothing outside it that could put pressure on it.

David: Everything is hanging in the Abyss.

Richard: It's floating in Space. At the same time it's totally stable. It's still. It can't fall anywhere because there's nowhere for it to fall to.

You will probably describe it differently. If my words don't do it for you, find your own, or just be with the non-verbal experience.

And you don't have to figure it out to see it. In fact, I don't think you can figure it out. This is unlearning rather than learning. Unlearning. It's being simple enough to just look, like a child—like the child you were.

Dale: I like the way you are drawing attention to the obvious. It's always been overlooked.

One consciousness

Richard: Yes. You've never seen a second View. Where would you put it? I keep a second one just here, you know, hidden, for use when I need it…

Dale: Keep an extra one, spare!

Richard: A spare one, yes!

The only direct experience of the Eye is one's own. God is called the One. Here is our experience of the One. There is only one Consciousness. How obvious is that! We hear about the consciousness of other people but it's hearsay, second-hand. You never directly experience their consciousness. Your only experience of Awareness is yours — you who are looking through this One Eye. And this Eye you are looking through is not a human eye, is it? It's divine. It's God's Eye.

The power to honour

Look ahead and be aware of your Single Eye. Notice that what you are looking at is in the centre of your field of view. Towards the edge of your View, the event horizon, things fade out. The View gets blurry. Now look at something else — now that's in the middle of the View and is most in focus. What was in focus a moment ago is now out of focus. Choose something else and now make that the centre of the field of view. You have the power to place anything right at the centre of the universe just by looking at it. Right now I make your face the centre of my world. You are right in the middle of the universe. Now I look at Mark and I make Mark's face central. Who is doing this? It's not Richard, it's the One. As the One you are promoting someone to the centre of the world. Only the One, only you, can do this. When you look at *me* doing it, nothing happens, but when *you* look at someone, that person appears in the centre of the world.

It's as if you as the One are a king or queen who is holding court. If you want to honour someone in your court you bring them to the front, in front of everyone else. In that moment they are honoured by being alone in front of the Monarch. They are bathed in your royal gaze! Then you send them back into the crowd and call someone else forward. As the One, when you look at someone you promote them to the centre of the world. Whoever you look at takes centre-stage. You honour them in this way. I am now honouring Joy. For this moment you are now at the centre of the whole universe. Never before this moment in just this way, never after this moment in just this way. Now I have promoted someone else—sorry Joy! So play! Make anyone or anything the centre. It's a respectful, honouring, beautiful, attentive thing. Wherever you look at someone or something you promote that person or object to the centre of the world. It's creative. Seeing is creative.

Chapter 5

Not Getting It

Alex: I'm lagging. I don't understand.

Richard: Well, none of us really understand. But can you see your face? No. That's the experience.

Alex: But everyone seems to be talking about something else, not directly about that.

Richard: Let me see if I can reassure you. What we are talking about are our reactions to not seeing our faces. We are talking about what this experience means to us. There are many different ways of thinking about it. That's why I said in the beginning that we all react differently. You might hear someone saying, 'That's amazing!', yet *you* don't find it amazing. If that's what you are thinking, I want to reassure you that even so you have got the experience — you can't see your face. That's the experience. So hopefully you can keep an open mind and then, during the day, see whether or not this comes to mean anything to you. Yes? The experience is that you can't see your face and we are going to look at this experience in a variety of ways.

William: You just described my first reaction. I didn't see it. I did the pointing and thought: 'This is silly. It's not working.' I tried it again. It was nothing. It wasn't, 'boom'. Then after a couple of days I tried the pointing again. Eventually it just sunk in, I can't really explain it.

Richard: We'll approach it from different angles and you can see what happens. At the end of the day, if it means nothing to you, at least you have hung out with some amazingly friendly people! And the coffee's good!

Chapter 6

The Card Experiment

Part One—The Mirror

Richard: We are going to do the Card experiment. Has everyone got a Card with a hole in it?

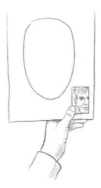

Hold your Card at arm's length and look in the mirror—you see your face there. The mirror reveals two truths. The first truth is what you look like on Sunday morning! I'm sure you're all happy to see a bright and fresh face there... The second truth is *where* that image is, *where* that face is—isn't it *out there in the mirror*, at the far end of your arm? I don't see a face here *at the near end of my arm*.

The mirror is showing you what you look like at arm's length. This is roughly what others see when they look at you from this distance.

Bring your mirror half-way towards you.

This is your appearance at this range.

Bring it closer—you see a huge eye. Make contact with the mirror—you see a blur. Now move your mirror back to arm's length.

Which of these appearances is you? Well, all of them. Each is you from a different range. Your mirror is showing you that your appearance changes with distance. Put the Card down for a moment.

If we could place a full-length mirror on the other side of the room you would see your whole body there. The mirror would be helping you see yourself from that range. What you would see there would be similar to how you appear to others at that range. There's a zone around you where your body manifests, in mirrors and in others.

Imagine a huge mirror about ten thousand feet up in the sky—you would see Levittown there. That's your appearance at that range—your urban face, your urban body. You need that layer—you need the water and sewage systems, the power grid, the roads and buildings… We can't exist as individuals without this greater body. Imagine looking in an even bigger mirror further away, say on the Moon—you would see the Earth there. That's your planetary face—manifesting at that range. At this close range you've got a human face, at that distant range you've got a planetary face. They are both your faces. We don't normally think like this but it makes sense to think like this. It's also rather wonderful to have a planetary face, a planetary body. You've got one, you might as well own it! You've also got a solar body. From several light-years you're a star! Even further away you have a galactic body. Why not say yes to your beautiful many-levelled body?

Carol: If you are having a bad hair day you can just say that you're a star!

Richard: Yes! It's amusing as well as beautiful. And it's also true. The mirror is a friend. It shows you what you are, not just at arm's length but, at least in theory, at more distant and at closer ranges. It helps us see this beautiful layered body we have.

Then the question is, 'What is at the centre of all these layers?' In other words, 'Who am I really? What am I at Centre, at zero distance?' Someone was telling me about an old song in which the singer sang something like, 'I've been to London and New York and Paris and Sydney but I've never been to *me*.' Well, this workshop is about visiting 'me'.

Why is it important to 'visit me'—to take a fresh look at yourself? Because you are your instrument for living. If you have a job to do, it's important to have the right tool. It's no good picking up a saw if you want to hammer in a nail. You are likely to hurt yourself. In the same way, if you are wrong about your identity, your tool for living, it's not surprising if your mistake hurts you and others. So finding out who you really are is important. Then the point is to live consciously from your Reality—not to remember it, or simply entertain the idea of your Self, or believe in it, or wish it to be true but actually to live it as a Reality. That's the thing—living it makes all the difference.

The question we are asking today is, 'What is my tool, my instrument for living? Who is at the Centre of all my layers?' The mirror and other people can tell you what you are from a distance—your beautiful many-layered body—but they can't tell you what you are at Centre because they can't get there. But you are at your Centre so you are perfectly placed to see what you are there. It's a well-kept secret. But all we need do to uncover this secret and see what we are at Centre is look there, which is what these experiments are about.

Part Two—The Hole

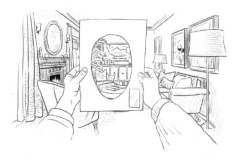

Look at the hole in the Card. It's a roundish hole. Because it's a hole you can fit anything inside it. Notice what is inside the hole now—a part of the room. The rest of the room is outside the edge of the Card.

Now bring the hole about half-way towards you and notice what happens—it gets bigger. More of the room fits inside it. Even closer and it gets even bigger. Keep moving it towards you and watch what happens—the sides of the hole get wider apart, the top and bottom then disappear.

Then eventually, when you put it right on, the Card completely vanishes and there's no boundary to the hole. Is that true?

No boundary! You have just guided your attention all the way home to this Open Space—this Open Space that is full of everything.

Keep your Card on and look round at the other people here. They all have Cards framing their faces and they all look silly, don't they? But there's one in the room who hasn't been framed, who doesn't look silly.

Jeffrey: Thank you!

Richard: It's true, isn't it? Have you been framed? No! Put your hand up if you don't look silly! [Everyone puts their hand up.] You alone haven't been framed, you alone don't look silly! You are not boxed in, you are not contained inside a Card or inside anything. You are free.

Jeffrey: What's neat is this remarkable contrast between the holes in other people's Cards which are filled in with solid things—their faces—and mine which is nothing, which is empty. Remarkable.

Richard: A complete contrast. How fortunate one is to be the one that isn't filled in! What luck! There's only one who can pass through this Magic Doorway into Heaven. Only one. You can't get to Heaven by being a person, you can only get to Heaven by being God. Only God lives in Heaven. Well, it's a metaphor, a picturesque way of putting it. Hold the Card out again. Who can pass through this Magic Doorway into boundless Heaven? Bring the Card towards you and put it on. Who has passed through into this boundless Space, into this Capacity that contains this glorious universe? Only No-thing gets through. Only you get through. The others, those faces, don't get through. They get stuck there in the doorway.

Eileen: That's why the word 'vastness' is used so frequently because it is vast!

Richard: Yes, it's a good word for it.

Eileen: No boundary.

Richard: Isn't it lovely to celebrate this together with different voices.

Here's a magic trick you can perform—you can make the Card appear out of nowhere. Take the Card off. It comes out of nowhere. How cool is that!

Unconditionally open

Let's do this experiment again. Look at the hole. It's a roundish hole. It's fairly small. Because it's empty you can fill it with anything. I'm fitting the floor into it, but now I'm fitting a person into it, now a picture. It doesn't refuse anything. It doesn't say 'No' to anything. It doesn't say, 'I'm going to say 'Yes' to the floor but 'No' to that chair.' It is built open. Unconditionally open.

Slowly put the Card on. Now the Card has vanished. All that remains is this boundless Space. You are seeing that the Space where you are is unconditionally Open. You are unconditionally Open for everything you are experiencing.

Now take the Card off. You are still unconditionally Open.

Putting on immortality

Ian: I look in the mirror and that guy is getting older.

Richard: But this One isn't.

Ian: This One is always exactly the same.

Richard: Isn't that wonderful.

Ian: It's a relief. I'm more worried about him, the one-in-the-mirror!

Richard: You should be! The one-in-the-mirror has wrinkles — well, for most of us, not for all of us! But this One has no wrinkles. This is the best cosmetic surgery — removes all wrinkles in a flash! The one-in-the-mirror was born and will die. In fact we learned we are mortal. Do you remember the first time you realised you were going to die? Some people do. You realise you are mortal. You put on that mortal face you see in the mirror and overlook your central immortality. Throughout the rest of your life you are under the impression, the delusion, that you are mortal. But now we can see that at Centre we are not mortal. Now we can live our fragile, mortal, human lives from this immortal Source! Fantastic. Now we can look in the mirror and say, 'Thank God I'm not like that!'

The Journey Home

We'll do this experiment one more time. This is a unique journey — from the region of your appearance to your Reality. You are travelling home to who you really are. Slowly put the Card on. As you watch the hole coming towards you, you are moving your attention with it, back towards the place you are looking out of. Keep looking. Don't mind what other people see, they are out there looking at your appearance whereas you are here looking at your Reality. When you bring your attention all the way home with the Card, you see that you do not look silly to you. You know you look silly to the others out there but here you are clean, clear, open, free, boundless, full of everything. Don't get talked out of your spaciousness, your immensity, your immortality, your wealth. Don't let others talk you out of your incredible nobility. Your True Self is boundless, timeless, wealthy, powerful, beautiful. We get talked out of the truth, we give away our power, we let others tell us who we are. Now we are taking back our power in the simplest way — simply by looking and continuing to look. You are balancing the feedback you are getting from others with your experience of who you really are. You are Open. Nothing sticks. If someone says you look silly, now you can say, 'Well I look silly to you *there* but *here* I don't look silly. What you say about me doesn't stick *here*.' Is that true?

Teresa: Absolutely. How you see me is *your* problem.

Richard: Yes, it is. Or my joy.

Now you are Home. You have taken that incredible journey from that region where your appearance manifests to your central Reality which is still, silent, safe, open, full of everything. This is the greatest journey — from something that was born and will die to that which was never born and will never die.

Now you see who you really are. You've got it. You can't not get it. You get it completely — you can't half get it. And no one can get it better or worse than you.

Teresa: Good bye!

Richard: Good bye! Yes, that's it, you've got it. Really! You can go home now.

This is not primarily for understanding. Understanding is important but primarily this is about experience. Your True Self is always available. It is what you are. It is free. It is very kind because it doesn't hide itself. If you want to hide your True Self, put it in the most obvious place — the place you are looking out of! Who would have thought? You say, 'It can't be true!' Alright, test it! Have a look and see if it's true or not. Don't believe me. Don't believe anyone — look for yourself.

Chapter 7

Closed Eye Experiment

This experiment explores who we are with eyes closed but we will start this experiment with eyes open. Be aware of your Single Eye. Be aware you can't say how big your Eye is because you don't see a second one to compare it with. And your Eye doesn't have anything around it — it's not contained inside something bigger, it's just hanging magically in Nothing. The View fades out all the way round into Nothing. Be aware of these two aspects — your View is the only View so you can't say how big it is, and it isn't inside anything.

Destroying the world

Close your eyes. The room has disappeared. You experience darkness. How big is the darkness? I don't find a second one to the right or the left to compare it with. There's only one. True? Is the darkness contained inside anything? No.

Open your eyes. What changes? The view out changes from darkness back to the room but the view in doesn't change, does it? In the outward direction there's the room and this way, looking in, there's Nothing. Let's do the two-way pointing gesture again — it helps bring our attention to these two directions. That way is the room and this way is Nothing. When your eyes are closed, that way is darkness but this way there's still Nothing. Close your eyes. Now there's darkness there but Nothing here. Open your eyes. Now the room re-appears in the Nothing. Magic! The view out changes but the view in doesn't. When I close my eyes I destroy the room, when I open my eyes I re-create it. You say, 'Richard, you're just closing and opening your eyes.' I am for you, but from my point of view I'm magically destroying and re-creating the room. Close your eyes — gone! Open your eyes — back again! You can make things appear and disappear.

You might ask, 'What's the use of being able to do that?' I say, 'Publicly it's of no use at all, but privately it confirms my identity. It's an inner thing. It confirms to me who I really am. Ah yes! Here is one of my powers!' So, exercise your power and destroy the room! Now re-create it!

When you awaken to who you really are you awaken to the truly astonishing fact that you are the One. You can't get better than being God! You are the One, you are Being. It should make the hairs on the back of your neck stand up. 'Being' is a small word for this incredible Mystery and Reality that you are. It's so great yet it's so humble because it's nothing. It becomes great by being humble. It's true, isn't it? The only way you can come to this Great Glory is by being nothing.

Sounds

Close your eyes again. Be aware of sounds. You can distinguish between different sounds. You can hear my voice. Now you can hear someone moving on a chair. You might like some sounds, you might not like others. Some are loud and some are soft. As I listen carefully I can hear fainter and fainter sounds. Finally there's a region where I no longer hear anything. There's an 'event horizon' there. Beyond the faintest sound is a place where you hear nothing. Or you could say that you hear Silence. Of course, Silence is a word for something that isn't a thing. It's No-thing, Capacity, Consciousness. All the sounds you can hear are flowing through this Silence, or are coming out of this Silence, or dropping into it.

How big is the whole field of sound? There isn't a second one to compare it with, is there? There's only one field of sound.

Is the whole field of sound contained inside anything? Not in my experience.

Are the sounds happening in a different Capacity from the Capacity the darkness is in? No. The sounds and the darkness are happening together in this one boundless Silence, Space, Consciousness. The sounds and the darkness are within you.

You don't have to understand this or think about it in any particular way. The experience is non-verbal, non-conceptual.

Open your eyes. The sounds are still occurring in the Silence, aren't they? All the sounds are within you. So when you hear my voice and then—let's have a little conversation as an experiment—you hear Dale's voice...

Dale: Hello there, Richard!

Richard: Both voices are in you, aren't they? Because I've grown up identifying with Richard and not Dale, I know this is my voice and that's Dale's. But now that I am seeing who I really am—and hearing who I really am—I am aware that both voices are mine. I'm enjoying having two voices! [People laugh.] Now I have many voices!

You are including others. You are being others. You are not just seeing others within you, you are hearing others within you. Many voices in One Consciousness. This is a different way of listening. It's an inclusive listening. It is such an interesting Nothingness—it's an alive Nothingness, Capacity, Silence. You are not just becoming all these colours and shapes, you are becoming all these sounds as well, moment by moment. You are speaking with Richard's voice now. It's fun! And all the sounds you are hearing are mysteriously, magically, arising out of the Silence where you are and dissolving back into it. Without you knowing how, or being in control, or making any effort.

Dale: I appreciate how you express that. That picture up there on the wall is Zen art—pine trees in mist. That is the Zen expression of what you are pointing to—those pine trees come out of the mist.

Richard: Yes! It is all coming out of the mist of Nothingness, isn't it! What incredible creativity! As the one-in-the-mirror we are more or less creative according to whatever society deems being creative is. Painting a picture perhaps. Alright, that's great. But as this One you can't stop creating! Everything is coming out of you, out of the 'mist'. Fresh, effortless, surprising, new, from every direction.

Let's go round the circle and say our names. Saying our names is an opportunity to hear our many voices arising within the one Silence. You are speaking with many voices. It doesn't have to be a 'wow' experience, by the way. It's a natural, normal thing. So, enjoy.

Here we go — Richard… [Everyone says their name.]

Dale: Like an orchestra.

Richard: Isn't this fantastic. This is a different way of hanging out with your friends. You are enjoying being them. This opens up the world again. Anyone you speak to, someone in a shop or on the street, your wife or husband, your children, you can embrace them in this deep, non-interfering way — because the way you become others is by being Nothing. You don't become them by imposing yourself. You make way for them, you disappear in their favour.

Charles: That really resonated when we had our eyes closed the first time and we were listening and then you said to open your eyes. Then all of a sudden the sounds and the room blended together.

Richard: It all blends, doesn't it?

Sensation

Close your eyes again. Be aware of your body sensations. Some sensations you like and some you don't. Some are in the foreground, some are in the background. Some are strong, some are faint — you are only just aware of them. Then beyond the faintest of all the sensations is a region where you feel nothing. There again is the Nothingness. The Space contains the sensations. It's a kind of alert Numbness that holds this boundless field of changing sensation — holds it, is it, is not separate from it. I can name this sensation my hand and that one my head and that one my toe, but that naming is going on in the Nothing too.

How big is the whole field of sensation? I don't find a second field of sensation to compare it with. Do you? No.

And I don't find this single field of sensation given within a bigger field. I don't find it inside something else. It's in the Nothing, in this boundless, shapeless Capacity.

This field of sensation is happening in the same Capacity as all the sounds and the darkness. It's all happening together in One Consciousness.

We identify with our body sensations. So if I say that I don't know how big the field of sensation is, I could as easily say, 'I don't know how big I am. I am not contained inside anything. I am boundless. I am floating in Nothing, appearing and disappearing in Nothing. I am emerging miraculously out of the 'mist'.' These are words. The experience is non-verbal so you can describe it as you like.

Open your eyes. You are still aware of your body sensations. The field of sensation—is it happening in a different Capacity from the colours and shapes of the room? There is only one Capacity. Can you say how big the field of sensation is now, with your eyes open? Is it contained? Mine isn't. My body sensations merge with the room. I am big, I am at large. Is that true for you? Being at large is very good for your body. It's being natural. It's healthy. This is how you came into the world as a baby. Growing up we learn to see ourselves from outside and we contract—we steal all our sensations from the world there and hoard them in a 'box' here. Then we wonder why we feel stressed. But now I'm re-awakening to my point of view and re-discovering my sensations are everywhere. The world is filled with sensation. The world is alive. I am at large, undivided from the world. Everything is arising in this One Space, this Awareness. There is nothing outside me, beyond me, up against me.

Be aware of your breathing. Where is your breathing happening? Is it inside something, contained in something? Isn't that rhythm happening in Aware Nothingness? If you say it's in your body, where is your body? In the field of view? And where is the field of view? Floating in Nothing! Isn't your breathing happening within this boundless awake Capacity where you are? Isn't it within the One, within this mysterious, indescribable Nothingness, Silence, Emptiness, in this Space in which everything is happening?

David: It was amazing then, when you brought everything into perspective. But when you said, 'Be aware of your breath', using the word 'your' shrunk everything. But then when I removed the word 'your', there was just breath. Sensation. When you take out words like 'my', 'yours', 'I', it becomes part of the Whole View.

Richard: Yes, I understand. But can I challenge you on that? Be aware of your breathing—no, sorry, be aware of 'breathing'—in the Space. Now be aware of the word 'the'. The word 'the', the sound and the image or whatever it is, is in the Space, right? Now the word 'your'—is it in the Space?

David: You got me. Yes.

Richard: So using a word doesn't stop you being aware of the Space.

Within this Consciousness, one moment it might be a sensation that comes to the foreground, to the centre of my Awareness, then in the next moment a sound or something else, bubbling away, appearing and disappearing. But this Consciousness, the Space in which this is all happening, doesn't change. It is constant.

Alex: I find it's easier for me to see that I am at large through vision and hearing than with body sensations.

Richard: I suggest you hang out with the bits you find easy and let that awareness gradually filter through into the bits that seem not to be so easy. That's part of the joy of it all, the adventure—it doesn't all fall into place at once in terms of understanding. It's a gradual unfolding for all of us. But boy!—when you start to say yes to the simple truth that you are at large, that your sensations blend with the world, it's so healing, so liberating, so healthy for you physically.

Thoughts and feelings

Close your eyes and be aware of your thoughts and feelings. Count to five slowly. Imagine the numbers appearing in the darkness. Now remember what you had for breakfast. Now think of someone you care for and be aware of your affection for them. Or think of a problem in your life and what you feel about it. Thoughts, images, feelings—changing all the time. Some you like and some you don't. Some appear big, some small.

Now attend to the whole field of thinking and feeling, to what we might call 'the field of mind', or more simply, your mind. How big is it? I don't find a second one to compare it with. I can't say how big my mind is.

Some thoughts and feelings are clear, in the centre of your field of attention, whilst others are vague, somewhere around the edge. Some you might just catch a glimpse of like a dim flicker of light. Perhaps you have a vague memory. What was that? You can't quite remember. Vague thoughts and images at the very edge of your mind. Then beyond that edge you are unaware of any more thinking. Out of range. Or you could say, beyond the faintest thought is the region where thinking fades into no thinking, into No-mind. All this mental activity is arising and happening within this boundless No-mind, Awareness, Silence. Do you have to stop thinking to experience this No-mind? No! It is where your thinking occurs. Just as sounds are arising magically from this Silence, so your thoughts are emerging out of this mysterious No-mind, out of this infinitely creative Blankness. Then they dissolve back into it. Thoughts do not obscure the No-mind, they happen in it.

Are your thoughts and feelings separate from the rest of your experience, from the rest of the world? You hear the traffic. Along with that sound you might have an image of a car, arising in the No-mind. Is your mental image of the car in a separate Capacity from the physical sound? Not in my experience. Both the image and the sound are going on in one Capacity. Is the sound 'out there' whilst your thought about it is 'in here'? Attend to the thought of the car. I find no dividing line between my image of the car and the sound of the car. Now you can hear a bell chiming. Are your reactions to the sound of that bell separate from the sound of the bell?

These words make it sound complicated whereas the experience is simple and self-evident. When I say that all this is going on in this one Capacity, in Consciousness, it makes it sound as though there are two things — Consciousness and what is happening in Consciousness. But there aren't two things — only one. But because we've got the experience we don't have to worry too much about the words we use.

Open your eyes — re-create the room in the Nothingness! Along with the colours and shapes in the Nothingness, and the sounds and the sensations, are thoughts and feelings.

Aren't your thoughts and feelings, along with your sensations, merging with the room? My thoughts are not in any kind of container here separate from the room there. My thoughts about the carpet are not here in my head, separate by a few feet from the carpet. The carpet, my thoughts, feelings, sounds—all are going on together in this one headless Space. I say I am thinking, but I could as easily say it's the room thinking. Or the One thinking. It's interesting to see what the One is thinking, isn't it? You are observing the changing thoughts of the One like the changing weather. The room is alive with constantly changing thoughts and feelings and sensations. They are popping out of Nowhere, aren't they? The whole thing is springing out of Nowhere without anyone pulling the strings.

We have regular online video meetings. This morning someone was saying that thoughts are like rain. That's brilliant—because rain isn't inside me, it's out there in the world. So that image indicates that the world is saturated with thinking and feeling, that the thoughts are out there, not in here. Here in the Space it's dry! No rain here. It's a beautiful image—the world is drenched in thought and feeling! It conveys the idea that it's a living, thinking, breathing, feeling world. The universe is alive. A living universe would be a thinking, feeling, breathing universe, wouldn't it? I now verify that it is!

Mark: Seeing who you really are is like holding an umbrella up under the rain.

Richard: Yes! The umbrella of your True Nature! It keeps you dry. There it's raining, but because the rain doesn't affect your True Nature it's not a problem in the same way. The world is drenched in feeling and thinking. Your thoughts about me now are blending with me, right? Yes. Your thoughts about what's going on now are in the room. It's the workshop thinking and feeling. This is a different way of thinking about things. It frees you to think in new ways. And it frees thinking from the box you'd imagined it was inside—the box of your head. This liberation of your thoughts opens you to being more creative. You see your thinking and your reactions are emerging in the No-mind—you are Open, you are coming out of Nothing. The No-mind is thinking now and the No-mind is unlimited.

Children know that their mind is at large. Well, they haven't yet learned that it is boxed away, separate from the world. As a child you do your thinking in your exercise book—until you learn you're supposed to do it here in your head. It's easier to think out there in your exercise book—less cluttered. There's more space there. It's more difficult to think in the tiny space of your head. Let your ideas arise in your exercise book, magically—let your writing happen out there on the page. Let your ideas unfold out of the No-mind as you talk—you don't have to have everything ready in an imaginary mind here. Your mind is not here anyway. That's the problem—thinking it is here, in your head. No. There's Nothing here—this incredibly creative Nothing. Out of this Nothing comes the universe, drenched in thought. It's raining thoughts—poetic, beautiful. It's raining thoughts. It's a damn tornado today!

If it's raining you don't take responsibility and give yourself a hard time—'It's my fault it's raining.' When you realise your thoughts are like rain, out there in the world, then they are not your fault. It's raining thoughts. Of course you have cloudy thoughts and sunny thoughts, and you prefer the sunny ones, but when you *place* your mind, when you see *where* it is, that it's *there* and it's not central, you are free of it. Then your mind breathes a sigh of relief. It loves you for letting it go back to where it belongs. It says 'Thank you' when you let it be where it is. Where is your mind? That's the question.

A friend of mine, Colin Oliver, wrote a poem about this –

Thought-Bees

If thoughts were bees,
who would dare to shut them
tight in the hive of the head?

He who shatters
this hive of pretence
with the swift hammer of seeing,
sees no box, no house,
no door to lock.
The spell of images is broken
and the swarm
breaks out
to scatter in the world.
The hive of nothingness
brings to the world
the honey of love,
and thought-bees,
watched by the queen
of the eye, roam free.

If you keep your thoughts in your imaginary head, it's not surprising if they get angry, like confined bees. Smash the imaginary hive with the swift hammer of Seeing! Out into the world the thought-bees fly. They are no longer imprisoned, no longer buzzing madly inside the hive. My thoughts are at large in the room. My thoughts are out there with the stars. That's where they are located. My feelings are at large. I am at large.

Chapter 8

Never Disturbed

William: When I'm aware of the Space, a very strong thought doesn't have the same effect.

Richard: It doesn't disturb the No-mind, does it? It cannot disturb the No-mind. It's not that you've got the No-mind going strong — it just does not get disturbed. So you relax. You say, 'Okay, it doesn't affect the No-mind. I don't have to somehow protect the No-mind or keep it clear. It's always clear.'

William: Sometimes it feels as if the thought is very big, like when I hold my hand right up to my face. It's bigger than everything else in the Space.

Richard: When you do that and your hand is as big as the room, does your hand interfere with the Space on your side of your hand?

William: It's not pleasant.

Richard: No, it's not pleasant, but it does not affect the Space. True?

William: True.

Richard: The idea that your True Nature is free from disturbance is reflected in the great spiritual traditions. Taoism refers to the bull's horn that can hook into things but cannot hook into the Emptiness. What on earth are they talking about? They are talking about the Space you are looking out of because nothing can hook into this Space. It's not because you've developed your practice so that finally things don't affect your True Nature. Things never affected your True Nature but now you are aware of it.

Mark: Because of my past meditational experiences with gurus I always have a lot of expectations. I have a mind which thinks, 'This should happen and this should happen', and if I don't see that, I think maybe it's not the real thing. So how do you deal with a mind like mine?

Richard: A mind like ours! Well, this two-way pointing gesture indicates the two views — in to the Emptiness and out to what fills the Emptiness. In this inward direction you don't see those expectations or anything, do you?

Mark: No, but my mind is still there.

Richard: Yes, the mind is part of the content of this Space. It's happening somewhere there, in the Space or No-mind here. This is meditation—you attend to the way things are in the moment, including whatever expectations are there. It's not primarily a matter of getting rid of your expectations but of seeing you are free of them here at Centre. We are bringing our attention to this place, to this No-mind, the Source of the mind, out of which these expectations come. The point is not to overlook this place of Freedom and No-thought—even whilst you are thinking or expecting things.

Mark: Yesterday night when I was in my bed I thought, 'Let me do an experiment. Be in this Space.' Suddenly this Space started expanding. Then the mind came in. Arghh!!

Richard: I know, but there's nothing wrong with that. That's all coming up in the Space. Be aware that those thoughts are coming up in this Space. Just keep being aware of the Space which is not affected by the thoughts.

Dale: I have read a lot in the different traditions and spent a lot of time practising. They all have their great ways of speaking about this point but I think the problem is that you are always hearing somebody else's experience of this. So we get influenced, thinking we should be having something similar to their experience. I think that's the biggest mistake because this is so immediate. Some people get angry, some people get elated, but when we were pointing back and our attention was just resting in the Clarity in and of itself—that never comes and goes. But everything that you can name does. That's the thing. That story that other people were promoting, saying you should have this or that, isn't actually what is really being pointed to. That story is an experience, a content that rises and ceases and this is the Ceaseless. It is really quite beautiful. Then you can make sense of some of the experiences after the fact, if this becomes the primary experience. All those things come and go. Sometimes we are focused outwards on the finger or the experience and it's a peak experience, but it passes. Then we think that we have lost this. But you can't lose this. That's the joy of this, the mystery of this.

Chapter 9
Insecurity and Safety

Roger: Could you say more about the safety side of it because I can get to that place, yet there is still this underlying fear. I would be delighted to feel safe but that feeling is not there. Then I think, 'Feelings are just within the Space and so on', but could you say more about this?

Richard: Yes, the feelings are in the Space. Even that deep underlying uncertainty is in the Space and does not affect the Space—which is always full of something. Now, every time that a feeling of insecurity comes up you can check to see whether it affects the Space. Apply that ongoing Awareness. This is meditation—it's not about avoiding something or trying to get rid of it or suppress it, it's about attending to it as it is given in the Space. You don't even have to know what something in the Space means, you just attend to it in the Nothingness. You hold it in the Nothing that never changes and see what happens. Now you have a place to host that uncertainty. That uncertain feeling is understandable because from the moment you were born you have been told to identify with the one-in-the-mirror and obviously the one-in-the-mirror is deeply vulnerable. Feeling insecure is understandable because uncertainty and insecurity underlie your life. It would be odd if you didn't feel insecure sometimes. It's an appropriate feeling to have.

This needs to be acknowledged because when we feel that basic insecurity we think there must be something wrong with us. 'How come I'm feeling this and no one else does? There's must be something wrong with me!' But no. Feeling that basic insecurity is actually appropriate sometimes. And you cannot solve that basic insecurity at its own level because as a person you are vulnerable, you are liable to all kinds of accidents, and you will die. We know that. Don't deny what is real at that level. But now we have also awoken to the level that is free and safe. Now we can view, entertain, welcome, host that insecure feeling within this Safety that is not dependent on anything.

This is not a way of suppressing or manipulating feelings, it is seeing *where* feelings are. You are the Space in which that insecurity happens. Test it. Seeing doesn't necessarily dissolve your anxiety right away, so if you are applying the Nothingness to anxious feelings and they don't immediately go away, know that you are not doing anything wrong. Just stick with it. That's the meditation — two-way attention. This is practical in the sense that it's simple and clear and you can do it immediately. It's not denying what you feel or pretending you don't feel something. You are acknowledging there's a very good reason why you might feel anxious. But now you are also seeing that there is more to you than your vulnerable human self. You are the Space in which all that is happening. There is no vulnerability, no anxiety in the Space.

Roger: About what you just said, Richard — that the vulnerability and insecurity is natural. Society says you have got to feel good all the time and when you don't, when you are feeling these natural feelings, there is a tendency to feel that there's something wrong with me. I realise today that this whole experience is not about feeling good, it's about accepting whatever is, in the moment — just bringing attention without judging. Just observe it, just bring meditation to it.

Richard: Two-way attention.

Roger: And it changes.

Richard: This is a journey of discovery, it is not a prescription. This is discovery. Now you have got the key to open that Door and walk through it and find out what happens rather than thinking about what you have read and what should happen and trying to make that happen. No. You've got the Master Key now. When that insecure feeling arrives, use the Key. Look at the feeling from this Open Door. Then have the adventure of finding out what happens whilst having the experience that you are basically safe.

Roger: It takes a lot of the strain out of it when it's not self-improvement, when it's about self-discovery.

Richard: An adventure is much more fun than a programme.

Chapter 10
Passion and Detachment

Carol: Don't emotions get less intense when you realise you are the One? You don't attach to the story, the story is not attached to emotions. It's not as intense. I feel more disconnected, not more connected.

Richard: I think everyone is different. I find my life gets more intense. I feel more passionately—yet at the same time I am looking from this Freedom, this Detachment. It's a paradox. When you see that you are built Open and you are Safe you can take more risks.

Henry: I didn't hear what you said.

Richard: Fundamentally you are Open and Safe, aren't you? This allows you as a human being to take more risks and to trust more because you've got the safety-net of who you really are. If you didn't have this safety-net you would become more and more careful as you grew older. But when you see who you really are your life gets wider and deeper.

Barbara: I thought I would feel less intensely about things. I feel more intensely about things but I react to them differently. For instance if someone I love dies, I'm not going to feel that less. I am not going to care less. But the reaction and the way you frame the story that goes with it changes with that consciousness.

Diana: There is less suffering because you accept it for what it is. You are not feeling it less deeply, you are feeling it differently.

Richard: Yes, well put.

Chapter 11

Fear of Nothing

Eric: I am angry because there is nothing here. There is nothing here. I'm shaking. It is just pure mind, it is just nothing. Am I right? I'm getting overwhelmed.

Richard: I think I know what you are talking about. It's overwhelming sometimes. I don't know if this will help but in my experience it's clear that this Nothing is always full of something. It's never just Empty. So when we say Empty we should really say Empty-for-filling-with-something. It's the limitation of language. The experience itself is non-verbal. When you look at me you don't see *your* face—and at exactly the same time you see *my* face. So your Nothing is always full. It is filled with everything, to the stars. And it is aware. The idea of Nothingness is scary but the actual experience is that it is full and aware.

Eric: I am seeing that there is Nothing and I am bringing everything into it to make it okay.

Richard: The primary thing is attention to the way things are rather than trying to manipulate things to be okay. To me, the way it is given before I try and change it to make me feel better is that it isn't just Empty, it is also Full. It is given that way whether I like it or not.

Eric: Does it matter one way or the other? I am trying to rock it.

Richard: Very good. Yes, really shake it. We are not here to deliver a comforting message for the sake of it. We are here to be awake to the way things are given and then with humility accept the way things are given, and then find out whether it works to live from the truth rather than from a lie. I can only speak with authority from my own experience. My experience is that this Nothing is Full and there's no dividing line between this Nothing and what's in it. In language it sounds like there is 'Nothing' and there is 'something' but in experience they merge. It's not two. I find no dividing line between the Nothing and the Something.

Kevin: Everything you experience is you.

Richard: What we are doing here is directing our attention to who that 'you' is. Society is always reflecting back what you look like and telling you that you are the one-in-the-mirror, which of course is true from society's point of view.

Jennifer: What I imagine in my mind, that is what I look like to myself.

Richard: Exactly. But then we take a fresh look at what we actually do look like to ourselves.

Chapter 12

The Four Stages of Life

I'm now going to suggest how the experience of headlessness fits in terms of the developmental stages of our lives. There are potentially four main stages in our lives: the baby, the child, the adult and the seer.

Stage One — The Baby

In the first stage of the baby you are headless, at large, Space for the world. You have not yet developed awareness of three basic aspects of the world — space, time and consciousness.

Space

Your field of view is kind of oval, isn't it? You can't see anything around it. If you look at anything, the thing you are looking at is in the middle of the View. It is most in focus. Then as you become aware of the rest of the View, objects get vaguer and vaguer until finally you can't see anything. I'm talking about your actual view. This View, your Single Eye, is all you knew when you were a baby. As a baby you don't yet have a concept of anything existing above the top edge of the View — for example the ceiling. You are not yet aware of things existing beyond the left edge of the View, or the right edge, below the View or 'behind you'. You are not imagining anything 'behind you' — a wall for example. All you see 'behind you' is the Nothingness. The only physical space that exists for you is what you are actually seeing — the View, hanging there in Nothing. Nor do you have any idea of a head where you are, a body right at your Centre. You are transparent. When someone walks past you, they don't walk past 'you' — they vanish into the Great Void. Then someone else magically appears out of the Great Void! You drop your toy and it disappears off the edge of the world, into the Great Abyss. Then your mother retrieves it from absolute non-being!

Pre-verbal, you didn't think in these or in any terms. Obviously I am an adult, a seer, describing this experience, but my own awareness now of the Space where I am enables me to understand my experience as a baby since in a fundamental sense nothing has changed. I am the same headless Space now as I was then—the View still floats in Nothingness. Even though as an adult I 'know' about the rest of the world that I cannot see, my knowledge does not change the essential experience of being headless, of being at large.

Time

The idea of time, of the past and the future, was also an idea you had not yet developed. You were only aware of now, this present moment—no before or after what is happening now, just now and now and now. Again, my own awareness as a seer that my Being is not in time enables me to understand the timeless condition I experienced as a baby.

Consciousness

Awareness of 'self' and 'others' go together. To become aware of myself I must develop the ability to put myself in your shoes and see 'myself' through your eyes—because my appearance doesn't exist here at my Centre, it manifests at a distance in 'others'. As a baby I have not yet developed this ability to go out of myself, turn round and look back at myself. When I look at someone I don't yet see myself from their point of view. I don't yet understand that they are a separate consciousness over there in that body, in that head, looking out through those eyes at the world and at 'me'. I haven't yet got the idea that they are seeing, hearing, thinking. I experience 'others' simply as appearances in my Consciousness. 'Others' are no more conscious than the floor is conscious. I don't yet think of a 'you' over there in that body looking at a 'me' in a body over here.

Because you don't feel looked-at, you look unselfconsciously. If you were a baby now and we put you in the middle of the circle of people here, you wouldn't feel that twenty people were looking at you. None of those eyes are yet charged with consciousness, peering at you and judging you. So you have no thoughts yet about others seeing you, no reactions going on based on the idea you are being looked at. Whatever feelings you have are not yet in the 'box' of your 'head'—they are floating around the room, in the air as it were. Unselfconscious, you are just looking. After gazing at a face you might then look past that face at a shadow on the wall and it's just as interesting. The shadow is no less alive than the face. The spontaneity of your behaviour is unrestricted by any thought of what 'others' might think.

You started your life in this condition, as this wide-open Space. You were not yet in the world, the world was in you. Neither were you yet in time. And you were not yet a 'self' amongst 'others'—the world was not yet divided up in this way. In a sense there was only your Consciousness—you had not yet learned there were 'others'. You as the One had not yet become 'one-amongst-many'.

Infectious

Continue imagining you are a baby. You are the Space in which everyone is happening. You are not self-conscious. You experience yourself being at large, Open. When you look at any face you take in that face without feeling self-conscious. You are broadcasting your Openness to everyone around you. Your Openness is infectious. Non-verbally you are giving everyone around you permission to be Open with you, without any effort, without words. As an adult you might turn from talking to a mother to making faces at her baby. You start speaking 'baby language'—'Goo, goo'. Then you turn back to the mother and return to your adult conversation—'You have a lovely baby!' You have just travelled from one stage of consciousness to another and back. Then you turn back to the baby and lose your head again—because the baby hasn't got a head for itself, there's no barrier. One reason people love being around babies is because their Openness is catching. When you look at babies they invite you to be headless with them. The baby is infecting you with its Openness. Non-verbally the baby is saying to you, 'I'm headless, I'm wide-open, come and join me, come and be headless with me.' Because it's got no face for itself, it's not feeling looked-at by you. It's looking at you but it doesn't yet understand that your eyes are seeing. It's not feeling under inspection. It's lack of self-consciousness is an invitation to you to drop into the Openness with it. We were all born in this infectious condition—broadcasting Openness.

The mirror

Look in the mirror on the Card. Imagine you are a baby and you are seeing a baby's face there—your face when you were a baby. But that's not you. It can't be you because it's *over there* and you are *here!* And it's small whilst you are boundless—you are nothing like that! You haven't yet put that face on here at your Centre. If your mother is looking in the mirror with you then you see two faces there but you don't think of one of them as yours. Neither of them is anything to do with you.

Sensations

You don't yet think of your 'body sensations' inside a body here separate from the rest of the world there—you don't yet know about 'inside' and 'outside'. Before you have learned to imagine your face and body here at your Centre your sensations are not contained inside anything. They are floating around in the room, they are at large in the Space, 'in the air' as it were. Be aware of the sensation of your forehead. You can't see your forehead. On present evidence how wide is that sensation? For a baby it could be as wide as the room! Where is it? It's rather hard to place—somewhere near the fan? What colour is it? No idea. When you as a baby are looking at someone's face, you feel your sensations 'here' but you don't think of them inside a 'face' here separating you from the person there. Both your sensations and that person's face arise together in the Space. It's the same with your experience of tastes and smells and sounds—they are neither inside nor outside you. Everything you experience is arising in the Space where you are.

Stage Two — The Child

In the second stage of the child you are becoming more mobile so you are increasingly able to explore the world on your own. And you are beginning to understand language so you are starting to take in the way adults see the world. Childhood is the transition period between the baby who is unaware of 'self' and 'others' and the adult who is convinced he or she is a separate 'self' in a society of 'others'.

As a child you are beginning to identify with the-one-in-the-mirror — you are learning to put on your human appearance, to take responsibility for the person you see there. At the same time you are beginning to understand that 'others' are real. A momentous change is taking place — the transition to being a separate person instead of being the Space that contains everything, and the transition to seeing others as also separate and aware and not simply as 'pictures-in-Consciousness'. You are joining the 'human club' whose entrance fee is accepting that you are your appearance and others are real.

Along with this growing awareness of self and others goes a growing awareness of space and time. As you begin to see yourself from outside you begin to see yourself placed against a background, and this background is growing as your knowledge of the world increases — from the immediate background of the room (that others see you are in) to your town, country, planet, star... You learn to place your actual View, which has no background, within these larger and larger backgrounds, colouring in, as it were, what is beyond the edge of your View. Now you 'know' what is above and below your View, or to the left or the right, or 'behind you'. Now you also 'know' about what came before this present moment and what might come after it — the past and the future. You are learning to locate yourself in time.

The mirror

As a child you are finding out which appearance is yours, which 'box' you are in, which body you are inside. Hold the Card at arm's length again and look in the mirror. Although as an infant you see the face out there in the mirror, you are in the process of learning that the infant there is 'really' at the near end of your arm, at your Centre. You are learning to put that appearance on, to put on that face as if you are putting on a mask.

There are tricks you are taught to play with the mirror that enable you to put your face on and become a person, a member of the 'human club'. Imagine doing the following — reach into the mirror, get hold of the face there and pull it out of the mirror towards you. Stretch it to make it bigger — it's far too small. Then flip it inside-out like a rubber mask because it's facing the wrong way. Then put it right on — stick it onto your central Nothingness. As well as imagining putting the image of your face on the Space here, you must also imagine putting the image of your whole body on the Space here.

Jennifer: Especially women.

Richard: In a different way from men perhaps but men do it just as thoroughly. You have to. As a child you are finding out through others and the mirror who you are in society. We all take that identity and put it on like putting on our clothes.

When you are an infant, adults look in the mirror with you and tell you that the infant there is 'you'. The job of the adult is to teach the infant to put that appearance on. Growing up involves developing the habit of imagining that appearance at your Centre — seeing yourself as others see you. Increasingly you ignore and suppress the Space, this undivided Consciousness that you are.

Marrying image to sensation

When you are looking at someone, at their face, you are learning to imagine your own face at the same time. You are learning to be 'face-to-face' with others. This involves learning to clothe the invisible sensations you feel 'here' with the image of your face.

Look in the mirror and touch your chin. Be aware of the sensation of your chin at the same time as you see the image of your chin in the mirror. I experience the sensation I call my chin some-where *here* but I can't *see* my chin here — it's a sensation without an image. In the mirror I see the image of my chin but I don't feel any sensation *there*. So I see the image in the mirror there and I experience the sensation somewhere here. During infancy and childhood I learn to imagine transferring that image there in the mirror onto the invisible sensation here. In the process I have to flip it inside-out and enlarge it — so it's the right way round and big enough. I'm learning to think and act as if the image of my chin is here. Though I don't see it here, I 'know' it is here.

Stop looking in the mirror but keep touching your chin. You no longer see your chin. As a child you have to learn to keep the image of your chin in mind so that the sensation becomes clothed with the image even whilst you're not looking in a mirror. You are learning to wear your face all day long. Touch the back of your head. Though you don't see the back of your head, you have an image of it. As a child you probably looked at photographs of yourself from behind or saw others touching their heads — from these observations you learned to clothe the sensation with the image. Obviously this is a smart thing to do, otherwise you'd bang your head on low doorways!

As children we are learning what we are for others, which 'box' we are in, which body we are in. There it is in the mirror — that's your body, inhabit it!

Empathy

Learning to map the image of your body onto your sensations means you can then relate to 'others'. I'm looking at you now and at the same time I'm imagining my face here, clothing the sensations I'm feeling with an image. Then I carry out a similar process in terms of my understanding of your experience. I see your face but I don't experience any sensations there, but because I've learned to attach an image of my face to the sensations here, I now imagine sensations over there in your face. This means I can imagine or empathise with how you feel. So when you smile

I know what that feels like because I've seen the image of my smiling face in the mirror, and I'm aware of the sensations that go along with that smile in the Space here. Because I know what a smile feels like here I can imagine the sensation of your smile over there in you. Without the skill of transferring the image in the mirror onto the sensation where you are, you would not be able to empathise with others. When you see me smile you know what it feels like because you too have married the image of the smile in your mirror with the sensations you feel in the Space — so when you see me smile it's almost as if you feel my smile. You are not feeling my smile, you are 'empathising' with me. You are imagining yourself in my shoes — in my head, in my body.

Imagine you are an infant and your brother is sitting next to you. You love pinching him because he jumps and makes a funny face! It's fun to watch. Until he does it to you… It hurts! And he says, 'That's what it feels like. Every time you do that to me I'm going to do it to you.' You soon stop pinching him. In that moment you have learned that he feels sensations in his body. Before then you had no developed sense of that. After this experience, this 'lesson', you still can't feel what someone else feels but now you accept that they are feeling something. It's the same with seeing. You have no direct evidence that the eyes in all these heads in this circle of people actually see. As far as you know they are just 'pictures-in-consciousness'. But as you grow up you learn that these people are looking at you because they tell you that they are. They tell you that they can see you. And they tell you that they can see your eyes and that you are looking out of your eyes — your two eyes — like they are. They insist you are not looking out of one boundless Opening, out of a Single Eye, you are looking out of two small 'windows'. They also tell you that your thoughts are inside your head.

A separate mind

The only thoughts you have ever experienced are your own. On present evidence where are your thoughts? You cannot see your head so you don't see a container for them at your Centre. There's nothing there to keep them in. You could say they are at large in the room, couldn't you? They are floating about in the air. Or you could say they are in Awareness, in the Space — which also contains the room. When you were a baby and a young infant you experienced your reactions out in the room. They were part of the view out. Your feelings and your body sensations were at large. Growing up is learning to centralise these things, to separate them out from the rest of 'the outside world' and imagine them inside you, in your head here, in your body — because society tells you that your 'mind' is in your head, your feelings are in your body. When you get the idea that your thoughts are inside your head then you get the idea that other heads must have thoughts inside them too.

As a young infant you are not yet aware of other minds. There's a test psychologists do to see if an infant has matured to the stage where she accepts the 'reality' of other minds. The psychologist gets a box full of pencils and shows the infant what's in the box. Imagine you are the infant. You see the pencils in the box. Then the psychologist closes the box so now you don't see the pencils, but of course you know they are in there. Then someone comes in the room and the psychologist asks you, 'Does that person know what is in the box?' You say, 'Yes.' You know what's in the box so you assume everyone knows. As far as you are concerned the idea of the pencils inside the box is out there in the room, in the air, it's common knowledge, a public fact. Because you know, everyone knows. Six months later the psychologist takes you through the same process. The box is closed but you know that this time there are coloured blocks inside it. Someone then comes in the room and you are asked if that person knows what's inside the box. 'Of course they don't,' you answer. Your reply demonstrates you have now taken on board the idea that there are other minds in the room. Now you are taking on the view that you are inside your head, inside your body, and that others cannot see what you are thinking and feeling.

Your thoughts are not 'out there' in the world where everyone can see them, they are hidden away inside your head—your head which you are convinced is there at your Centre though you don't see it. So now your 'mind' is private. Your knowledge of the coloured blocks is 'yours', it's 'in your head'. Now you are beginning to have an 'inner life' that is yours alone, that no one else has access to. You are beginning to realise you can keep secrets or even tell lies because no one can see your thoughts. You are beginning to realise you are separate. At the same time you are beginning to understand that 'others' are in the same condition—they are inside their bodies and you can't see what they are thinking and feeling. They are separate like you.

Flexible identity

Being inside your body, becoming a separate individual, is a learned thing. You are not born in a body, you are not born separate. You have to learn about your body and learn to get into it and learn to act as if you are in that body. As a child you are finding out which body you are in—you are learning who others see you to be, who you are in society. But you keep forgetting—forgetting you are the one-in-the-mirror. You have to be reminded that you are in that body, that you are separate, that there are other minds, that there are 'others'. 'You are not the only one here! You are not the centre of the world. The world doesn't revolve around you!' But you keep forgetting. Your default position is there's just one mind—yours; one field of body sensations—yours; one consciousness—yours. Your default position is being unaware of your appearance, being open to the world—living unselfconsciously from your original Openness. Because it takes time to learn that you are in the particular body you see in the mirror, as an infant you could just as well be in any 'body'. So it's as easy to be a train or a car or a lion as it is to be a boy or a girl. And a lot more fun! You experiment with different identities. Often you forget you are in any 'box' or body at all and run around 'headless' and 'bodiless'! This is a very free, open, spontaneous, creative, playful stage in your life.

Infectious

Whatever stage of consciousness we are in is highly infectious. We know how infectious the baby's consciousness is—if we had a baby here it would non-verbally be saying to everyone here, 'I am headless, you are headless.' We would all feel that, respond to that. It's hard to resist the Openness of a baby. If we had a child here it would also be non-verbally broadcasting its consciousness but it would be communicating something different from the baby: 'I'm trying out being in a body but I haven't quite got into any particular body yet—come and join me in my freedom, my flexibility. I'm going to let you out of that one human box you are in—now you can be anything. During this time together we are going to be all sorts of things and we can change and be something different whenever we like.' The child gives you permission to make things up as you go along, to be anything. This flexibility and freedom is something you know well because you were once a child.

If you had a child here and during the coffee break he asked you to play with him at being trains, you would feel fine about getting down on the floor and being a train. All the other adults would understand. The child would be giving you, the adult, permission to be a train. But when the break ends and the child goes off to play somewhere else you would stop being a train. If you continued on your own, more than a few eyebrows would be raised!

Two-way communication

All communication is two-way. I am in you and you are in me. At the same time as the adult is being given permission to be a child, being infected with the child's fluidity and Openness, the adult is teaching the child to abandon that basic Openness and to identify with the one-in-the-mirror—to become an adult. Whilst the child is giving me permission to be a train, I am inevitably communicating to the child, 'This is just 'playing', it's not real, it's a pretence. You are not a train. The 'reality' is that you are a boy or a girl playing at being a train.'

Behave yourself

Imagine you are a child and are running around being an aero-plane—as far as you are concerned you are flying. Your jet engine is making a lot of noise. But there are adults around who are not playing with you. You bump into one of them and he's annoyed and snaps at you: 'Behave yourself!' Suddenly you are confronted with the fact that you are not 'really' a plane, you are a child, a person. In that moment you morph from being a plane to being a little boy or girl. You stop running around—you stop flying. You are no longer a noisy plane. But a few moments later you've forgotten you're a child and you're a plane again...

Until the adult again tells you to 'behave' and you morph back again into your human body. You have become 'self' conscious again—conscious of being a person. Childhood is a learning period in which you are experimenting wearing a body, learning to inhabit a body. You are not yet tied down to the body-in-the-mirror so you experiment being in many different bodies.

Abandoning your openness

But increasingly as time goes by you settle into the body that society is telling you is yours. Increasingly you overlook or forget or deny your headlessness, your native Openness.

It's vital that you abandon your Openness and take on a body—the body in the mirror. You have to play the game of having a face—the Face Game—and you have to learn to play it so well that it's no longer a game but is 'reality'. Otherwise there's no way you could function in society—you would probably need institutional care. But in fact you're happy to play this 'game'. You want to 'play', you want to join in, you don't want to be left out. This is the only 'game' there is. You don't want to remain 'a baby', you want to 'grow up'.

Angela: There were some moments in my childhood which a psychologist might consider as traumatic experiences. I remember in kindergarten a girl running by me and banging into me. She hit me on the nose and it hurt. I started to cry. But prior to that moment

I think I was in the headless state. I think the trauma was not this little girl hitting me and me crying, I think the trauma was being knocked out of that headless state.

Richard: That makes sense. We all have to go through the trauma of being knocked out of the headless state into the 'headed' state. We all get shrunk from being Nothing and Everything to being one little thing.

Believing in others

Kevin: You say that when you develop, then you understand that other people are thinking. I think that you don't understand that, you believe it.

Richard: Yes, I believe it.

Kevin: You develop a belief system. I don't understand that you are thinking, I keep developing the belief system that there's someone there looking at me. But I don't know this. I don't know it at all. There's some kind of barrier that prevents me from ever knowing what you are doing or even if you are there. We develop a belief system more than an understanding. It may even be a lack of understanding.

Richard: Yes. I understand what you mean!

Kevin: I know you do! [Laughter.]

Richard: Yes! But if you don't take that belief on board you can't join society because people are then just 'pictures-in-consciousness' and there's no one there or here. In that sense you would be alone and 'society' would be no more than an idea. It would have no meaning for you.

Stage Three — The Adult

In the third stage of the adult I identify profoundly with the one-in-the-mirror. The mark of being an adult is that you look in the mirror and you don't think twice about that being you. You know it's you. I believe profoundly that I am my appearance, that I am the one I see in the mirror, that I am at Centre, at zero inches, what you see me to be from several feet away. Accepting I'm face-to-face with others, I 'know' I am separate from everyone.

Infectious

This stage is also infectious. When I believe and act as if I'm in a body here, then I treat you as if you are in the same condition there. The underlying 'truth' I live by is — 'I'm in a body, you're in a body.' The baby's experience is — 'I'm not in a body, you're not in a body.' The child — 'I'm not sure which body I'm in yet. Come and be anything you like with me.' The adult — 'I'm behind a face here and you're behind a face there.' Seeing myself in this way, I see you in the same way — and you take in my message. When I look at you, you feel looked-at by me. I am communicating to you what I see you to be. I am telling you by all manner of verbal and non-verbal signals that you are a thing, a person. Not only do you take in my message, you give it back to me. When you look at me I also feel looked-at — I am aware of myself as a person in your eyes. You only have to look at someone and you are communicating to them that you are a person and they are a person. We are now supporting each other, helping each other maintain our awareness of and our identification with what we look like. We are saying to each other, 'My consciousness is behind my face here, your consciousness is behind your face there. We are face-to-face, we are separate. My sensations are contained in my body, your sensations are in your body. My thoughts are here in my head, your thoughts are there in your head.' In the third stage of the adult you have come a long way from when you were a baby and had no developed sense of yourself and others.

Denial of who we really are

In adulthood my deep acceptance of the reality of self and other is accompanied by the denial of the reality of my Spaciousness, of who I really am. If someone refers to headlessness, as an adult I reject the idea. 'What do you mean I'm headless? That's mad! Of course I've got a head! I'm a thing here, not Nothing. I know

I can't see anything here but I know my head is here.'

Fear of not being

When you are a teenager and finding out who you are in society, the last thing you want to be is a nobody—you want to be somebody. You don't want to be left out. You don't want to be the last one chosen for the team. We need to belong, we need to be accepted, we don't want to be rejected. So the idea of being nothing, of being a nonentity, a nobody, a loser, is seen as the worst possible thing. Not knowing what to say, being lost for words, not knowing who you are or what you are good at—we dread these things. You've got to find out who you are, get on with making the best of yourself, move fast, avoid losing time. We understand this drive to be somebody. It's appropriate and healthy as we are growing up to develop ourselves, to become somebody, to succeed. But it's not surprising if within us lurks a fear that we will slip and tumble into the abyss, the darkness at our Centre—the Nothingness we are doing our best to get away from. And whether we think much about it or not, we know that in the end we die, that all we have achieved and have become will vanish. If we scratch the surface deep enough, non-being stares back with a threatening eye.

As good as it gets

Society tells us that the third stage of the adult is the final phase of development. This is what life is all about—growing up is about finding out who you are as an individual (you have no choice about who you are born as), and then taking responsibility for that person. According to society that's it, more or less. There isn't another stage in the sense that you can't become someone else, you can't radically change your identity. This is it. This is as good as it gets. Now your task is to make the best of the cards you've been dealt. And then you die! We are at a Buddhist centre here—you've got to get death in! Now that I identify with the one-in-the-mirror, when that one dies, I die. And that's it. According to the social view, I've gone. In the end all I hold dear turns to dust. It's understandable if I can't see the meaning, the purpose in life. What is it all about?

Stage Four—The Seer

But the third stage of the adult doesn't have to be the end of the story. Potentially you can move on to the fourth stage of 'the seer'—being a person *and* being the One that contains everything. This is being fully grown-up, fully mature. You haven't fully grown up until you have awoken to being the One.

In disguise

Now you are aware both of your appearance and your Reality. You are the One, but you are the One in disguise. Why do you laugh?

Graham: It's true!

Richard: Yes, you are the One in disguise as Graham. Secretly you know you are the One—you are not Graham, you are everybody else! But you still take responsibility for and act as if you are Graham. You are both. We are now sharing a secret because from the outside no one sees your headless Nature. It's a private experience. It's a secret. Yet everyone experiences this clear open Space where they are—so we are sharing this secret. Although I am manifesting as Richard and you are manifesting as Graham, we are both now aware of being the One. We are sharing this wonderful secret.

It's like being a king in disguise in your own country. In stage three you didn't realise you were the king so it wasn't your country and these were not your subjects. But now, although you've awoken to being the king, or the queen, the One, you still appear as an ordinary person. No one else can see that you are the One. It's fun that people don't know who you really are. Except they do! They do and they don't. But you keep your persona going. You are in disguise. You are the One in disguise as a person.

Infectious

In the third stage you subscribe to the belief, 'I'm in a body, you're in a body.' That's highly infectious. Non-verbally I am transmitting to you, 'I'm in a body, you're in a body, we are separate, we are face-to-face.' In the fourth stage you are aware of being headless, that you're not in a body. This fourth stage is as infectious as the other stages. In the moment of being conscious of who you really are, you are transmitting your headless Reality loud and clear to everyone around you. You cannot fail to transmit that Consciousness. At the same time you're still aware that for others you are in a body and you identify with your body. So you have two things going—you are aware of having a two-sided identity. You are not regressing to being a baby who is headless but is not yet aware of itself as separate. You are now aware of both your Reality and your appearance. On the one hand you are conscious that your 'little self' is out there in the 'movie', it is one of the characters. On the other hand here is this open Space where you are free of the 'little one'. You still identify with your appearance, I'm sure. I do. But that's okay, that's part of the 'movie'. You are now broadcasting both identities—'I'm a person and I'm not you and you're a person and you're not me', AND 'I am Space for you and you are Space for me'.

Self-consciousness

You are now seeing who you have always been. Now you find out what difference this Seeing makes in your life. For example, take the feeling of being looked-at by other people, feeling all those eyes are observing you—feeling self-conscious. You can be aware of this happening now in this group. When I look at you, you feel looked-at. I only have to look at you and I'm non-verbally communicating, 'I see you, you are a person.' I'm reflecting your appearance back to you. That's why people don't like being looked at sometimes because they feel self-conscious, under inspection. They feel they are being solidified, made into a thing. You know the myth of Medusa, the Greek goddess who had snakes instead of hair? You couldn't look at her because if she caught your eye you would be turned to stone. The hero is Perseus and his task is to kill her. This is a myth that relates to what we are talking about because in the third stage of the adult, when you are not yet aware of your headlessness, looking at eyes makes you feel looked-at, you feel self-conscious—those eyes turn you into a thing like Medusa turned people to stone. When you've been turned into stone it's called being 'petrified', which also means being scared out of your wits. Every eye has the power to turn you into a thing, to petrify you. How did Perseus kill Medusa? He didn't look at her directly because he knew that her eyes would kill him, so he looked indirectly by looking in his shield—he used it like a mirror—and then, seeing her reflected, chopped off her head. Your True Nature is the shield, the mirror—this Clearness is like a mirror—it's clear yet at the same time you see the world in it, perfectly reflected. When you look at someone and you are seeing your Clear Nature, you see that their eyes don't make you into a thing. You are No-thing. Even though you may feel self-conscious, at the same time you see that you remain Transparent. You are not solid, not a thing right where you are.

Whenever you feel anxiously self-conscious, now you can apply the remedy of consciously being this transparent Space. This can help in those moments when you feel so under inspection that you freeze up, when you feel you cannot be yourself. Apply this remedy. And be patient with yourself—things take time to untangle. When Perseus had killed Medusa he put her head in a bag and took it back to the king—the bad king who had given him the task of killing her. The king looked in the bag to make sure Medusa's head was in there. But Medusa's eyes still had their power and the king was turned to stone. So, one look at your True Nature is not enough—other people's eyes still retain their power. You have to keep coming back home to who you really are, keep seeing that those eyes do not petrify you.

Remembering
We know where to look. Seeing your Original Face is not the hard

part, the hard part is remembering. These experiments are now bringing this Awareness into this group. You're realising you can see who you really are with others. In fact the very things that made me feel under inspection — other people's eyes — can now remind me I'm not under inspection. What puts us in the 'box' — in the box of our bodies and minds — is others. Now you can use others to take you out of the 'box'. When you're with others, get into the habit of noticing you're eyeless and faceless — face there to No-face here. Others become great pointers to who you really are.

Returning home

In the first stage of the baby I am Nothing. I don't know about being something. In the second stage of the child I'm Nothing but I'm learning to be something, to be somebody. In the third stage of the adult I've found out who I am in society. I've made my home, as it were, in my appearance. Now today we are re-awakening to the headless state, to our True Home. Because we've gone away from our headlessness, away from the Openness of the baby, coming back to it now has a special value which it would not have had if we had never gone away from it.

Laura: So today is a beautiful initiation back into it?

Richard: Yes, today we are being initiated back into our original True Nature. 'What does he of England know who only England knows?' What do you know of Home if only Home you know? When you come back to who you really are you can appreciate the Openness here in a new way — having been away from it. Now you see it with fresh eyes.

Laura: The Prodigal Son.

Richard: Yes. This idea can be found in various spiritual traditions. The journey away is necessary. Our lives are a wonderful story. We've been told that the book ends with chapter three, the stage of the adult, but suddenly you discover there's another chapter, the fourth stage of the seer. A whole new chapter! It was a brilliant thing that we left our True Home, that we closed the door on this secret garden, because now we come back to it afresh — back to the Home we never really left.

Two-sided

Sarah: I'm totally Open as who I am — if I totally accepted that, wouldn't I forget my public self?

Richard: I don't think it will happen because your identification with being a person is so profound. You'll never completely forget who you are as a person, you'll never completely lose it.

Sarah: You have two identities.

Richard: Yes. Does your awareness of being a person, of being Sarah, get in the way of seeing your headlessness?

Sarah: I don't know. I'll have to check it out.

Richard: Well, check it out now. Don't wait.

Sarah: Yes, yes, I'm doing it.

Richard: Can you see your head?

Sarah: No. I can't. Ah! I just got it! Ah! I got it!

Richard: You can feel deeply identified with Sarah and at the same time you can't see your head. Identifying with Sarah does not get in the way of seeing who you really are. In fact identifying with being a person highlights who you really are. Identifying with your self-image is a beautiful development in Consciousness. We're not trying to return to the unselfconscious baby.

You are both the 'little one' and the Big One at the same time. You are both. This is being Home, being who you really are even with all your faults. Home, just as I am. Like in the song Amazing Grace — just as I am, poor wretch — something like that. I can see who I really am just as I am, wretch though I am. The experience I'm talking about is simply noticing that you can't see your head. You don't have to think about that to see it. You just look. Can you see your head now?

Not fearing nothingness

This is directly experiencing who we really are. This is reliable. It can be tested. Now this changes the game, changes our lives. When you are growing up and finding out which identity you are, when you are going through your teenage years, you want to be somebody—the last thing you want to be is a nobody, a non-entity. In the fourth stage of life, the stage of the seer, we come to discover what real non-entity is. We see that the Nothingness at our Centre isn't just empty, it's also full—full of everything. It is Being. It is not this awful thing we were afraid of, lurking somewhere inside us, about to swallow us up at any moment. Loss, non-entity, nothingness, disappearance, not belonging—all this looks different when you see who you really are. Now we can be in the Centre where we don't need to be anything or know anything, where in fact we know that we cannot be or know anything, yet we see that we are alright. I AM—my Being is. I AM—both empty and full.

An amazing journey

Our lives are an amazing journey. At the beginning of your life you started as the One and were not aware of others—the headless baby. In adulthood you have been taught to be aware of others, to be aware of the many, and you have learned to dismiss the reality of the One. You had to go through that process to develop a profound awareness of self and others. Others are not just 'pictures-in-Consciousness'—you accept they are real. Though you cannot prove the reality of others you have the deep conviction that there are others here in this room—others who have their own thoughts and feelings even though you don't experience any of that directly. With every fibre in your body you act as if others are real and you are real—you as a separate self. Now, awakening to your private experience of being the One, you still have this feeling of others, you still are convinced of the reality of our public selves. Far from having to get rid of this feeling, this sense of the reality of 'self' and 'others' means that you as the One genuinely have the feeling that you are talking with others—you are no longer the 'only one'. There are 'others' to talk to about all kinds of things, including the fact that both you and they are the One! How wild is that! We are talking together here today and we can be aware that our many voices are coming from one Speaker, are happening in this one Consciousness. I am aware now that I am the One and you are the One and I am enjoying talking with you about this—talking with you who are both myself and not myself!

Chapter 13

The No-Head Circle

Stand up in a circle. Put your arms around each other and look down at your own body.

You see your feet, your legs, your torso. Then you disappear above your chest into this open Space you are looking out of—your Single Eye.

There are two sides to yourself—there's your body down there, and there's this clear, unbounded Consciousness looking down at your body. Yet these two sides of you are not separate. Your body is not separate from this Consciousness.

Look down at the floor in the middle of the circle. You can see the circle of feet, the circle of bodies. All the bodies fade out around chest or waist level — they all disappear into the same Space at the top that your body disappears into. Is that true? Are all these bodies coming out of the same Space that your body is coming out of?

You have just grown all these bodies! Down there we are many and different and at the top we are One and the same. There are no dividing lines in this Space at the top. You can't divide it up. All the bodies now are yours — they are all coming out of this Consciousness. You are not a part of this Consciousness, you are all of it. It is indivisible.

This is primarily seeing, not thinking. You don't have to understand it in any particular way. If my words don't fit for you, find your own or use no words at all.

It's also not a feeling. It is neutral. You don't have to feel the same way about it as anyone else. There's no right way of responding. You don't have to psyche yourself up for it. If anything, you have to psych yourself down for it!

All the bodies are coming out of this one Clarity. Down there we are many, we are distinct, we are different, and at the top we are One, the same. There are no dividing lines at the top, no names on this Consciousness, or nationalities, or ages. This is visible, obvious, sane.

Okay, let's sit down.

Isn't that incredible! What a great way of appreciating the Many and the One. And though we are back on our chairs and you can see everyone's face now, there is still only one Consciousness and it contains everyone. This Awareness validates multiplicity and difference. There in the group separation is normal and sane, here in the Space unity is normal and sane. We are not trying to impose unity where it doesn't belong. This Awareness frees us to be different, frees us to be the individuals we are.

Andrew: It is not the One *or* the Many, it is the One *and* the Many.

Richard: Yes. Now you are aware of this one Consciousness that belongs to everyone. Anyone who is not present here in this group is still this Oneness at heart. The child we can hear playing outside, someone on the other side of the planet, someone a thousand years ago, it doesn't matter—this Space does not exclude anyone. You include everyone and everything.

You are seeing this Space for everyone, aren't you? You include everyone, there is only One.

Chapter 14

The Sun of my Soul

This experiment addresses the mystery of the Many and the One from a different angle. It's called The Sun Of My Soul. First we'll do the No-head Circle again.

Stand up in a circle and put your arms around each other. Look down at your body. Notice your legs and torso and how your body vanishes into your One Eye. Your body is coming out of the One. Now look down at the floor and notice the circle of feet, the circle of bodies — they all fade out around waist or chest level into the One at the top. Down there we are Many, at the top we are One.

Drop your arms by your sides. Turn round so you are still in the circle but are now facing out from the centre. This is now The Sun Of My Soul experiment. You will start by holding out your arms. First I'll take you through the experiment quickly. Then you'll drop your arms so they don't get tired and I'll take you through the experiment again but more slowly, so we can go into things in a more relaxed way.

Open your arms in the shape of a 'V' so that you are embracing your view out. Between your hands is your view of the world, your unique view out. Let your arms overlap or underlap the arms of the people either side of you.

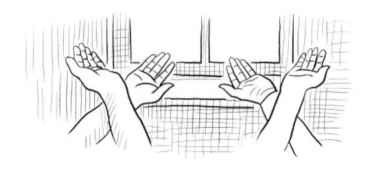

This indicates that what your neighbours see overlaps with what you see—perhaps the same window or chair.

You can also see that your arms come out of your One Eye, out of the Space where you are. At the same time you can see your neighbours' arms on either side of your View and they are also extending out of your Eye, out of your Consciousness. Now drop your arms. We'll go through it more slowly.

Your view out is yours and yours alone. Only you experience your View. Only you experience your thoughts and feelings, only you experience your life. When you talk with others you hear about their views out. You understand that their views out overlap with your view out, like their arms were overlapping with yours—you see the same window or chair, you are experiencing the same workshop. If there was no overlap at all you would have nothing in common with others to communicate about. But you never experience their views, you only hear about them second-hand. You accept everyone has a view out, but it's hearsay. So—you have your view out, your experience of your life, and when you talk with others you find out about their views out and how they overlap with yours.

Now be aware you are looking out from your Single Eye, from the One. You see that the one who is aware of your View, of your experience, of your life, is the One — it is the One who is now seeing, hearing, thinking, it is the One who is really living your life. Your life is arising within the One.

When you talk with others they tell you they are also looking out of the One. Their lives are also arising in the One, flowing from the One. Their descriptions of the One fit your experience perfectly — it is boundless, timeless, nameless... Yet each person has a uniquely different View arising within the One — each person's unique life is flowing from the One, just like yours.

You directly experience your own view out from the One, you hear about the other views out from the One. Many views from One Consciousness. This is a way of thinking about the mystery of the Many and the One. It doesn't explain this mystery, it paints a picture of it.

We can sit down now.

You see that your life is unfolding within the One. Now you understand that everyone's life is unfolding within the One. Jesus spoke about there being "many mansions in God's house". My view out is one of many views from the One Consciousness — it is one of the many 'mansions' within God's house. I experience my life unfolding within God. Then I hear about other people's lives, unfolding within God — other mansions in the house. Many mansions in God's house.

William: That exercise is so powerful because if there was only your view it would be tremendously claustrophobic and isolating. But to have your view within the context of the others!

Richard: Yes, what a beautiful thing. My view out overlaps with what you tell me about your view out. I can see that pattern on the carpet. Can you see it? You say, yes. Well, I trust that you can see it. I don't have your experience, I only hear you confirming you see it. But I respond as if you are seeing it. In that sense our views are overlapping. We have a different angle on it — that makes it interesting! On top of that, we are both looking out of Nothing so both my view and what I hear about your view are happening in the One. The fact we can both see the carpet makes communication possible. But our overlap there is a bit hit and miss because how do I know that what I see as red isn't blue for you? We can never know for sure that we see the same thing because what the other sees is hearsay. But we go along with it and it seems to work.

Now let's attend to the place we are looking out of. You can't see that differently from me. You can't see it a bit clearer. It's not blue or red, is it? It doesn't have a shape so we can't get the shape wrong. It doesn't have an age. This is perfect communication, isn't it? This is uniting. Only to have the view out is to be separate, however much we think we understand each other. We are in different bodies. But now when we wake up to who we really are—that's union, isn't it? Yes. Total union. At the same time we continue to have this precious sense of difference, of otherness.

Chapter 15

Movement

This experiment is connected with movement—you all have to run round the property ten times… I'm joking!

I'll show you what you're going to do—you're going to stand up, point at your No-face, slowly turn round and see if you move or the room moves. Not too much exercise! Stand up. Make sure you don't bump into anyone. Point at your No-face, look at your finger and slowly turn round. Of course, stop if you get dizzy.

Don't you see the walls and everything in the room moving past your finger? Is that true?

But the place you are pointing at isn't moving, is it? This is the difference between the outside and the inside. Looked at from the outside you turn round and the room remains still, but from your point of view it's the room that's moving and you remain Still. It's fun, isn't it? It's so simple. How easy this is to share.

You can notice this when you are walking, when you are driving. It's not a matter of thinking, 'I am still and the world is moving.' This is not thinking, it is seeing. So you can be thinking about which way to go down the road and at the same time have the non-verbal experience that the road is flowing through you. You are not manipulating your thoughts and feelings.

Notice something else concerning movement—you remember what I was saying about size? You can compare one thing with another thing—it's either bigger, smaller or the same size. Then you look at the Whole View and there isn't another Single Eye on the right or the left to compare yours with—there's only one Eye so you can't say how big it is. It's the only one. You can also look at anybody here in the group and see a boundary around them. There's something all the way around them. Then you look at the Whole View, at your Single Eye, and there's nothing around it. It's not set inside a bigger background. True? Yes.

Movement is also relative in the sense that if I move my hand you can tell it's moving because you can see it moving against the background. If the wall was moving at the same time and pace as my hand, then my hand would be still in relation to the wall. If you sway from left to right you can see something in the foreground moving against things in the background. Movement is relative. Now become aware of the Whole View. Can you move it to the left or right?

Angela: There isn't a left or a right.

Richard: There isn't a left or a right so you can't move it! Now I'm going to invite you to walk through the room and notice that things are moving about within the View but you can't move the Whole View. See if you can move the Whole View. There isn't a background against which you can see it moving. It's rather fun. Everything within the View is moving around like mad but the Whole View is floating in Nothing, in Stillness. Okay, we can sit down.

This is not an abstract idea, it's a concrete experience. However much you walk around you will never move the View, the Single Eye.

Brian: You are referring to the screen, the movie screen?

Richard: The whole thing, yes. Everything, including my body, my sensations, everything within my View is moving around but the Whole View—there's nowhere to move it.

Here's another way of thinking about it—you didn't come to this workshop, this workshop came to you. You never go anywhere. You have never moved an inch in your whole life! You are always at home—it's the decor that keeps changing!

Roger: I drive a school bus. It's a new thing. When I started driving I wasn't used to the big bus and I was tensing up. I was trying to get somewhere. But as soon as I was the Space I realised that everything was moving through me. I relaxed. My whole body relaxed. It was effortless, so simple. The old way—I was tensing up.

Carol: Typically during the course of my day, when I'm working and I'm driving, it's me moving forwards and it's very stressful. This practice gets me out of the driver's seat so that I'm more in the background. I'm receiving the scenery rather than bulldozing my way through it. It's a completely different perspective—less stressful, less driven. I would rather be more of a receiving person than a get-out-of-my-way person. It's like that. Receiving it all.

Roger: I love that phrase, 'coming back Home'. You get a sense that you are Home no matter where you are and you get that empowering stability feeling, instead of always running. It feels like you are always running and trying to find safety for most of your life. I was running, running, running. I would go on vacation and then I would feel I've got to get back home. No matter where I was I was depressed and miserable.

Richard: And now, when you are driving your school bus you are at Home and the whole bus is inside you!

Here's another movement experiment. Stand up and hold out your hands in front of you. You see your arms coming out of your Single Eye. They are floating there, stretching out from the Space. Move them around a bit — let your hands dance together. Because your arms are coming out of the Space, you can say that the Space is moving your arms and hands. You don't know what they are going to do next. There they are, dancing.

Now stand side-by-side with someone — put your inside arm around the other person so you are close and you can look out together in the same direction. Extend your outside arm in front of you so that your hand is near your partner's hand. I am noticing my arm coming out of my Single Eye, but as I look ahead I see my partner's arm is also coming out of my Single Eye — out of my Consciousness. Move your hands so they dance together. I've grown another arm! Isn't that weird? I'm not inside one arm more than the other, they are both in me. I am dancing with both hands!

Stand next to someone else and grow another, different arm!

Now we can sit down again.

Chapter 16

Distance

Richard: We're playing with this—you've got the experience. We are exploring the experience in different ways. This one is going to blow your mind—it's so ridiculously simple. You are going to use this Card like a ruler to measure the distance between two things. Pick any two heads in the group. Put one end of the Card in front of one head and see how far along the Card the other head is, along the 'ruler'. Simon is half-way along the ruler from Paul, but George is the whole length of the ruler from Paul. You get the idea. If you pick anything within the View you can measure how far it is from something else.

Now measure how far you are from one of those heads. Bring the 'ruler' round to measure from one of those heads to the place you are looking out of. The ruler shrinks to a point. No distance!

It's the same with the whole View—it's no distance from 'you'. If you say the View is 'out there'—out there from where?

George: Relative to what?

Richard: There's no reference point beyond the View.

Kevin: There is something immeasurable this way and it is projecting the View out there. From here it is the one View that is out there. That is sort of giving it a place, a location.

Richard: Yes, it's a paradox. It's very odd. We can't define this in words. It is no distance away and yet it looks like it is there, yet it is here.

Kevin: It's here and there.

Richard: We've covered all the bases!

Laura: The immediate experience doesn't feel like depth in that way. It's like the movie screen and the image. The image appears to have depth but in actual experience it doesn't feel like depth at all.

Richard: I think we can accept more than one description here.

Laura: Yes, but I don't feel that I am feeling that over there. It feels that I am knowing that exactly here.

Richard: I know what you mean, yes. I think somehow it's weird.
You can't pin it down. It is very weird.

Chapter 17

The Unclassifiable

This experiment involves me placing a small coloured sticker on your forehead! But before we go any further, there are several rules you need to follow. First, you're not allowed to talk during the experiment. Let's say there's something you don't understand about this 'game'—you can't ask! You can't talk until we have finished. Not talking is a difficult thing to do, even if you are all practised meditators which I'm sure you are! Not talking means you can't ask any questions. You have to tolerate mild confusion or frustration for about three minutes!

When I put the coloured sticker on your forehead you'll close your eyes so you don't see the colour. Then when you open your eyes you can't look in a mirror or other reflecting surface and you can't touch your sticker. Then I will explain what the game is about. Close your eyes. I'll come round and put a sticker on your forehead.

Part one

Open your eyes. This is the yellow area over here in this part of the room. Here is the silver area, here is the brown area, over here is the red area. Stand up. I am now going to count to five. This is the game—by the time I've counted to five all those with a yellow sticker on their foreheads have to be in this area, all those with a silver sticker come over here, all those with a brown one here, and all those with a red one here. I'm going to count to five. One, two... You have to move. Three, four... Go! Go! You must move! [People move.] Five.

Be aware of your reaction. You will have time to share your thoughts and feelings when we have finished.

Part two

If you are one hundred per cent sure that you are in the right area according to the colour on your forehead, stay there. But if you have any doubt at all, come to the middle of the room. In the game, if you stay in one of these areas and you are wrong, you lose everything, so to speak — all your money. But if you admit you don't know and come to the middle, you lose nothing. [Some people move to the middle, some stay where they are.]

Some of you have stayed in your areas so you must be one hundred per cent sure you are in the right place. Be aware of why you are one hundred per cent sure. And everyone who came to the middle, be aware of why you are not sure.

This is the red area. Everyone who is not in this area look over at the reds. If both these guys are in the right area, make the 'thumbs up' sign. If at least one of them is in the wrong area, 'thumbs down'. Okay you guys, be aware of how you react. Thumbs down! One of you is not red! Be aware of your reactions because they are showing 'thumbs down' to you!

Over here is the brown area. Come close and look at everyone in this group. If all these three people are brown, thumbs up, but if at least one of them is not brown, thumbs down. Which is it — thumbs up or down? Mixed messages! Some thumbs up, some thumbs down! You are not sure if one of them is brown or not? You guys in the brown group, be aware of how you feel about this feedback — the mixed messages.

This is the yellow area. Three people here. If you are one hundred per cent certain you are yellow, stay there. If you have any doubt at all, come to the middle. You are all staying put. Okay, if we can see that any of you are wrong, we put our thumbs down. Thumbs down! Two of you are moving to the middle of the room — that shows how powerful group pressure is! [The one who stays is the only one who is wrong!]

Being sure means being absolutely sure — one hundred per cent and not ninety-nine per cent. If you have any doubt at all about your colour, come to the middle of the room. [Some stay where they are and others move to the middle of the room.]

Part three

Now we move on to the last part of the experiment. There is a way of figuring out which group you should be in according to the colour of the sticker on your forehead. If you can figure it out without talking, looking in a mirror or touching your sticker, do it. [Some people move others to the various colour-coded parts of the room.]

If you are now one hundred per cent certain you are in the right area, stay there, but if you have any doubt at all, come to the middle. [Some move, some stay.]

Let's sit down.

We can talk now. What are your thoughts, your reactions?

Trusting others

Mark: I had to take other people's word for what colour I was.

Jennifer: I hoped that someone would look at me and say, 'You have to go there. Now you're in the right place.' I had to totally trust what their perspective was.

Richard: You were dependent on their feedback.

Jennifer: Yes.

Angela: I was a hundred per cent confident that I was brown because I was with my mom and I trusted my mom.

Richard: I can't argue with that! You trusted your mom. Yes, we trust our moms.

Angela: Even if it hadn't been my mom I would have had faith in other people to tell me that I was brown, that they weren't lying to me or trying to trick me.

Confusion

Nigel: Initially when we were told to go to one of the areas, I had an intuition about my colour. The second time, when you said, 'Try to figure out where to go', somebody pulled me over to the brown colour. Then when I was sitting here, people were looking at me as if I was in the wrong place.

Richard: It must have been confusing.

Nigel: I had an identity crisis!

Richard: It's a powerful experience, isn't it? You were confused because you got confusing feedback.

Nigel: Yes.

Not trusting others

Peter: I knew for sure that I would never be able to know the colour unless I saw it for myself, because for all I knew everybody in the room might have been cued in to tell me the wrong colour. So why should I trust anybody? Even my own mother, if she were here! She might have been part of the game.

Sarah: I was pretty sure because I had gotten some feedback as to where I should be. But then when you asked, 'Are you sure enough to risk everything?' I wasn't, because there's just no way I could be sure. Absolutely no way.

Richard: This doesn't mean to say that you can't trust people ninety-nine per cent, but I was saying one hundred per cent.

Sarah: Some people are colour-blind so you could have trusted someone who was colour-blind, who may not have known they were colour-blind.

Richard: So they might be wrong without knowing it.

Agreeing to play

Richard: In the beginning I said, 'By the time I count to five you must be in the right area...' What would have happened if you had all decided, 'I can't see my colour so I'm not going to move.'?

Barbara: We would have just sat there.

James: No game.

Richard: No game. If you want to play the game you've got to guess your colour or trust someone. If there's no game then there's no fun and no learning. Not moving would have been understandable because you can't see your colour, but there would have been no game.

Carol: The fact that we allowed you to put a sticker on our

foreheads indicated we had already agreed to play the game.

Richard: Yes. At that point you were all in the game already.

Eric: When you said, 'Go to your area', I didn't move because I had no way of knowing. There was no reason to move, no reason to go anywhere.

Richard: Did you move in the end?

Eric: One little step, over to the brown area.

Richard: Why?

Eric: Because you asked us to go to one of those areas.

Richard: Why did you do what I asked you to do?

Eric: I was playing the game.

Richard: Right! If you hadn't played there would be no game.

Eric: Right.

Richard: If there's no game there's no fun and there's no learning. Imagine you are an infant and your parents say to you, 'Smile for us, Mary'—or John, or whoever you are. Imagine you can reply in words and you say: 'I can't be one hundred per cent sure I am Mary so I'm not going to respond.' The result is that you don't participate in the interaction, the communication—you don't play the game of being human. To play the game of being human, the game of life, we have to trust others even though we can't be a hundred per cent sure of them. We have to trust there's somebody there inside each of those heads. There's no absolute proof there's anyone actually there. You don't feel my feelings so how can you be one hundred per cent sure that I have feelings? Growing up is learning to accept that you're there inside that body and others are there inside those bodies. I learn to trust I've got a face here even though I've never seen it here. This is learning to play the Face Game. The 'sticker game' is a version of the Face Game. I learn to trust you when you tell me I have a face here. I learn it so deeply I forget I've learned it. I think it's true. 'I am what I look like. Of course I am!' Then everything I do comes from that position, doesn't it? I act from the position that I am separate from you, that I am behind my face here and you are behind yours there. I'm in this body and you're in that body. If I don't accept this, I can't play the game, I can't participate as a person in a society of real others.

Working out the rules

William: I moved because I didn't know what else to do. It seemed to be the thing to do.

Richard: Yes, everybody else is doing it!

William: I didn't have time to really consider.

Richard: No, you didn't. I put lots of pressure on. I said, 'Go, go, go.' When everybody else moved you went with the crowd. When we join any group we try and figure out what the ground rules of the group are. In this workshop today you might wonder if you are allowed to go to the bathroom in the middle of a session. Are you allowed to have a second cup of coffee? Can you go outside? We watch what others do. We try to read the situation to work out what the unspoken rules are, what the right thing to do is.

Feeling stupid

Mark: I felt very uncomfortable. I still feel very uncomfortable because I feel I'm stupid or something. I thought I'd missed something in the instructions. I have no idea how anybody knew where to go. Generally speaking people were in the right place except for a few. I only went to the silver area because I used some kind of logic. I figured the colours were equally distributed. I only saw one silver so I figured I must be silver. But I don't remember you saying anything about the distribution of colours. I thought, 'I have no idea how anybody knows. How do they figure it out?' I feel very stupid.

Richard: Did you see some people moving others about?

Mark: No, I didn't see that.

Richard: You didn't see that! That's how people got into the right areas—other people moved them there. Now you understand how people got to the right areas.

Mark: Yes. That's what made me really uncomfortable. I didn't know how they found out where they belonged. How did they do that?

Richard: This is just what I was referring to, and it reflects our experience sometimes in life. When we grow up we join groups but we are not told the unspoken rules. We have to try and figure out what those rules are. Sometimes everyone seems to know what's going on except us. That was your experience in this game.

Playing at not playing

Margaret: It's funny because just now I've been thinking that clearly I'm very evolved because I didn't move. Now I realise that's what I've been doing my whole life — not playing the game. I'm just going to stand on the sidelines and think that I'm right and that you all are missing the point. It's annoying to hear that I'm supposed to be playing this damn game! I don't want to play. No! Like a little kid.

Richard: The game you're playing is, 'I'm not going to play!'

The mirror as a friend

Laura: I felt really uncomfortable. It's how I feel in life a lot, like I don't belong, like I'm making a mistake.

Richard: I know. It's very powerful, and it's just a game of stickers!

Laura: I was getting tense.

Richard: You felt you didn't belong because…?

Laura: Because I was getting mixed messages. That's how I am. I watch everybody else's reaction and then react to that all the time.

Richard: The only way you can find out what colour you are is by other people's reactions, isn't it? But you are confused now about where you belong, are you? Do you want to look in a mirror and see what colour you are?

Laura: Yes.

Richard: Look in the mirror.

Laura: It's orange! I thought I was red.

Richard: Yes, it's orange and not red. The confusion arose because the orange is similar to the red — it's hard to tell them apart. You might be red. But now, looking in the mirror has clarified to you why you were getting mixed messages from people. The mirror is really useful, isn't it?

Laura: It is.

Richard: Now you don't feel confused. Even though you don't belong to a group because there isn't an orange area in the room, you are not confused.

Laura: Right. I'm not confused any more.

One hundred per cent sure

Jennifer: Someone moved me into one of the groups and I trusted he was correct.

Richard: Who did you trust?

Jennifer: Anthony.

Richard: Anthony is such a trustworthy person!

Eric: I think Anthony actually moved someone into the wrong area!

Richard: Do you still trust him?

Jennifer: I have no reason not to trust him.

Richard: But he moved someone into the wrong area!

Jennifer: You don't know that for sure.

Eric: That's right, but I know that Anthony likes to play games. He's mischievous.

Richard: I said, 'If you are one hundred per cent certain then stay where you are.' Are you one hundred per cent certain that Anthony put you in the right area?

Jennifer: Yes.

Richard: One hundred per cent?

Jennifer: Yes.

Richard: How can you be one hundred per cent certain that Anthony isn't colour-blind?

Jennifer: Oh!

Richard: Oops!

Jennifer: Yes, oops!

Richard: It's a good job you were not betting money on this!

Jennifer: True.

Richard: I'm not saying that Anthony is not trustworthy. I'm questioning that you can be one hundred per cent sure that he can be trusted?

Jennifer: Okay.

You must trust others

Richard: As we grow up we get labelled by everyone around us. Growing up is like this game we've been playing—you find out who you are in society through others who you trust. If you don't trust them, then no game, no society. That feedback from others continues when you become an adult. It's going on right now in this workshop. You are continually getting feedback from others—everyone here is telling you who you are all the time, verbally and non-verbally. And you are accepting it. I only have to look at you and you feel looked-at. You are accepting that you are what I see you to be—a person. You can't see your face but if you don't accept that you are what I see—a person with a face—then you can't 'play'. You can't function in society because you would be refusing to accept your place in society as a person.

Belonging

Richard: When you were welcomed into a group by someone else, was that a good or a bad feeling?

George: A good feeling.

Richard: A good feeling. Ah, thank God someone wants me!

George: Exactly. That's over! I know where I am!

Richard: Yes, that's over. When you are a teenager you want to be accepted by your peers. You don't want to be left out. You don't want to be nothing and nobody, you want to be somebody. It's better to be anybody than nobody, isn't it? Did others have that kind of feeling when you were welcomed into a group—I'm all right now. I'm glad I'm not that poor guy in the middle who doesn't belong anywhere!

David: I felt really bad because when Kate came to our group, and I've known Kate for a long time, I thought, 'You don't belong with us.'

Richard: Yes. It can be hard to push somebody out of your group, to reject them.

Anne: I wanted to take the guy who was left in the middle and bring him into our group, no matter whether he was silver or not.

Richard: What was going on for you there?

Anne: I don't like it when somebody is left out.

William: I thought, 'Okay I'm not red, where do I go now?' My feeling when the other people said 'Yes', when they welcomed me into their group, was that I had figured it out.

Richard: So now you felt alright. This fits with what we experience as we grow up. At the beginning of your life you don't know which group you are in. Then people help you find out what you are. By the time you're an adult you're sure which group you are in—I'm a red and not a yellow so now I'm going to act as a red. I am a person, I'm not a bird or a train. I'm a boy and not a girl, or a girl and not a boy. Now I belong somewhere. Now I know how to behave!

William: Yes.

Richard: I need to know who I am in society. I trust others to help me find out. If I didn't trust others I couldn't function. But you can't be one hundred per cent certain of your colour because you can't see it. And you can't be one hundred per cent certain you are a person—with a face, like everyone else. But you trust people ninety-nine per cent when they tell you what you are, which means you can function in the game, in life.

What is certain?

Is there anything about yourself that you can be one hundred per cent sure about?

Margaret: Emptiness.

Richard: Yes. Point now at your sticker—you don't see your sticker there, do you? You don't see your face there. You see Open Space, right? Does awareness of that Open Space depend on others confirming it?

James: No.

Richard: The reality of your True Nature, that which is most you, the core of you, is not dependent on others confirming it.

Carol: It's self-evident.

Eric: It cannot be confirmed by others.

Brian: Can you say that again?

Richard: You need confirmation from others to know the colour of your sticker. You have to keep getting feedback from others to know who you are as a person. But when you point back at the Nothing, does it need me to confirm that you are that?

Brian: No.

Richard: In fact I'm not in the right place to confirm it. I'm in the right place to confirm you have a sticker, that you have a face, but I'm not in the right place to confirm your No-face. But you are in the right place, aren't you?

Brian: Yes.

Richard: Your True Self is not even dependent on you remembering it. I'm not asking you to remember it or believe in it or trust others to tell you what you really are. You can see your True Nature for yourself, here and now.

Trading faces

What do you see instead of your sticker?

Barbara: Everyone else's sticker.

Richard: Yes. From the outside you are in one group and are not in the other groups but from the inside you are not in any group, all the groups are in you.

Negative to positive

As we grow up we learn to repress our Nothingness. Because no one else can see our Original Face we learn it isn't real. Although I don't see my face, you tell me I have a face, that I'm separate from others, so I learn to distrust my experience and instead put my trust in you. I suppress awareness of this Openness. Sometimes as an adult when I have glimpses of my No-face I find it scary. I think I'm disappearing. Or perhaps I find myself not knowing what to say, my mind goes blank—I feel I should have something to say, that I must be somebody. I feel pressure from society to be something, to be a certain way. We learn to be frightened of the experience of being nothing, of being nobody, of being empty and blank.

Now that we are re-awakening to this Openness we can begin to appreciate this Nothingness, this unclassifiable Blankness in a new way. It is Being. It is the Space that contains everything. It shows I'm not separate from anyone, that I have your face now instead of my own. It is the gateway into connection. It is an infinite resource—it is coming up with ideas and thoughts all the time, all popping up out of Nothing. Sounds are all the time coming in and out of the Nothing. This whole day together is emerging in the Nothing—what a creative Space! Now I am appreciating that this which I was afraid of is a blessing. I'm Nothing and Nobody which means I am full of everything and everyone. At the same time I continue to know myself as a person—I am two-sided. I am Nobody and I am Richard.

Roger: I'm glad you said that. A while back you were talking about self-consciousness being okay. When I was first introduced to the headless way, to the Nothingness, I was almost trying to kill that self-consciousness.

Richard: You can't do it. Instead of rejecting it, now you welcome it. Now self-consciousness is part of the situation. It means you as the One can participate in the game, you can play your part in society.

Misunderstanding

John: It was interesting. I was watching Mary directing traffic there. That area was yellow but Mary was directing Sue there and Sue was red.

Mary: I didn't direct Sue!

Richard: I can see there was a misunderstanding!

Mary: You directed me!

John: Me?

Phil: Both of you directed me here but then someone else told me to go over there!

Richard: You guys directed Phil there?

Mary: I didn't. He did.

William: Awesome!

Richard: Isn't it interesting!

William: The directions are not always right.

Alex: People can be mistaken in the way they direct you. That's why your question is important — 'Are you one hundred per cent confident now that you are in the right group?'

Basing my life on a mistake

Richard: You get feedback from others but it's not always right. We are defenceless as babies and have no alternative but to accept what others tell us. The underlying message beneath all the messages, whichever sticker you are told you have, is that you are a person, you are in a body. You cannot be sure that others are right but what alternative have you but to trust them? So I learn to see myself as you see me, though you might be wrong. I might be basing my life on a mistake, a misunderstanding about who I am. In fact I am. I am living as if I am just my appearance, as if I am only what you tell me I am. The mistake I'm making is that I am overlooking who I really am. I am living a kind of half-life.

Not the end of the game

When you are a baby you don't know you are a person, but as you grow up you join in with what is happening and learn to act as if you are a person. You accept what others tell you because you don't want to be left out. Anyway there's no choice — not participating is not participating in life.

Then society says, 'You have now found out who you are in society. You are a person. You are John, or Ellen, or whoever.' You accept that the goal is finding out who you are — what colour sticker you have in this game, and which person you are in life. Once you have found out who you are you must take responsibility for being that person. You have to learn to act as if you are that one. That's the deal, the game. You have no choice about which person you are—you are the one you see in the mirror. You can't choose to be anyone else. So you play as best you can with the cards you've been dealt. And that's it. That's life, apparently. In the game, in life, you find out which sticker you have on and learn to act as if you are that one. Life is about making the best of the person you find yourself to be.

But finding out who you are in society need not be the end of the game. Potentially it is only half-way through your development. Generally people don't realise there's another part of the game, another phase of life. The next part is what you are doing in this workshop today—re-awakening to who you really are. Who you really are is not what *others* are saying you are. It is what *you* see yourself to be, so you have to stand up for yourself, you have to look for yourself. That is why a certain kind of defiance is at the heart of this workshop. 'I am not going to let anybody else tell me who I really am because they are not here where I am, so they have no authority to tell me what I am at Centre. Instead I am going to look for myself. I cannot see my sticker. I cannot see my face. Now what does that mean? I am unclassifiable! I am not in a body!'

At the same time, having no coloured sticker here I find that all the coloured stickers are in me. I see all the other colours instead of mine. I trade stickers, I trade faces, I trade identities. I am not in a body, all bodies are in me! But do I now stop playing the game of being in a body, of being a person in society? No. I continue playing that game but now with this inner awareness of who I really am. This enables me to operate even better as a person, with more compassion, more understanding, more strength. I discover a growing inner confidence because I am operating now from the fully reliable experience of what I am rather than from what you tell me I am—which I cannot be fully sure of. There is great freedom and creativity and safety in this. I am not in a body—I am not limited.

Deep down I am free! My world is emerging miraculously out of this Awareness—how creative my True Self is! And my Being cannot be harmed—I am safe. Totally safe. So we continue playing the game, the 'game' of life, but now in a profoundly different way, from a deeper and truly real and reliable base.

Boundaries

Peter: I will hang with that yellow crowd to be accepted because they all tell me they love me and this red crowd over here don't, or that, growing up, I am 'white trash'. I look at them and I think, 'I don't like none of them except the ones that accept me for who I am.' But I can't accept myself around that crowd. That's the fight, to accept me and not worry about anybody else's opinion.

Richard: I understand. But I suggest that what you might think about during this workshop today is that from your own point of view—Well, I'll speak for myself: I am not brown or silver or red or yellow or anything. That's my reality, even though you tell me I'm a particular colour. What colour am I? Yellow? So I accept I'm yellow in your eyes. I can't see my colour but I trust that you are telling me the truth. But you might be colour-blind so I can't be one hundred per cent sure. Yet I act as if I am yellow now because I am taking on board your feedback. But my inner truth is that I am not yellow or silver or anything. I don't have a face. I am Clear Space here. Therefore all the reds and the yellows, all the people who like me and don't like me, are actually myself. Now that might not be a pleasant discovery because I might prefer not to be some people, but it is the way things are. But seeing you are Space for others doesn't then mean that you let others walk all over you. Whilst you put your boundless arms around everyone, you still honour your own separateness. Being aware of my two-sided identity means in some situations I can say, 'Stay there! I am you but keep your distance! I am boundless but this is the line between you and me and I want you to stop there!'

Nothing sticks

James: I have become more open in the last six months than I have in my whole life because of trying to find out who I was. I was locked away in a cage inside my head for so long. In the last six months I have become open to both silver and red. Some days they still get under my skin. I am working at that, even sitting here. But just a year ago I would have said, 'You're a 'flake' man, get away from me.'

Richard: Okay. But the brilliant thing about this is, although I would have accepted that you saw me in that way, there is nowhere for that name or label to stick here at my Centre. No matter what anyone says, nothing sticks to your True Self because there's nothing here to stick it to. I look here and I see that no label sticks here. This is freeing. Obviously you will never get everybody to like you. There will always be things happening that you don't want to happen. But have a look and see if they stick. They don't. That's the simple truth. Even though I might feel hurt by what someone says about me, here at Centre the truth and reality is that it doesn't stick.

Dale: Very liberating.

Richard: It's your basic Reality. The basic Reality of who you are is unstickable. It's a technical term I found in a secret Buddhist treatise — 'unstickable'.

Peter: Did you say 'in the Buddhist treetops'?

Richard: I said 'in a Buddhist treatise'. But 'treetops' is better. In the Buddhist treetops!

Dale: Yes, the sticker can be placed there but not here. Beautiful.

Richard: Fact!

Dale: Never personal.

Richard: You just can't do it. It's not dependent on whether you are good at it or not or whether you understand it or not, it just doesn't stick. Seeing who you really are is accepting reality. A very beautiful, brilliant reality. No label sticks here. I am looking at you but my reaction to you does not stick there, does it? There's nothing there. That's freedom. But you are still open to my reaction. You don't have to deny or block out what I am saying. What you might say about Richard might be true—it's your view of me. But it is not who I really am. Fantastic.

You cannot prove your Unclassifiable Nature outwardly. From the outside all labels stick, at least to some degree. But inwardly nothing sticks. You are clear like glass. You are like a mirror that reflects everything but the mirror itself is never stained by what it reflects. Your face in the mirror gets dirty but your True Nature, your Original Face—never. This is practical. This freedom at your Centre is an observable fact. It's not because you have been meditating for ages or somehow are lucky or special or different. It is nothing to do with that. It is just fact, just the truth. You are looking out of this Open Space, this headless Space. We are all looking out of it. When you see who you really are you understand, you believe, that everyone else is also looking out of this Space. This makes sense. It's absolutely clean, clear, still, free—for everyone.

Communication is two-way

Diana: I was thinking about when I was in middle school, there was a girl who was the leader of the group. Everyone listened to her.

Richard: She was the authority.

Diana: Yes. Did that mean that she took on board that view of herself because everyone looked at her as an authority.

Richard: She was doing it to others as much as they were doing it to her. We are all doing it to each other. She was getting that identity reflected back to her but she was reflecting back to you that you were her followers. That was the deal. But even deeper than that, the underlying transaction is that you are a thing. I am a thing, you are a thing. Whether you are a leader or a follower, you are a thing. You are not 'Nothing-full-of-everything'. You are a thing separate from every other thing and things are limited, things are vulnerable, they get hurt, they die, and you can only be in one place at once and all that kind of stuff. That's the underlying, unstated message of all our communication.

When we awaken to This, you see you are No-thing. You are

not a thing. This Consciousness is as infectious as 'thinging' each other. I am looking at you now and I'm noticing that I am wide-open Space for you. In this group we have permission now, it's on the front burner, to be Space for one another. That's infectious. It is love. Basically it is love. It is receiving everyone just as they are given, within you. But does that mean now that we have stopped reflecting back who we are as people? No. Hi Phil! You see, to address someone is to reflect back to them who they are as a person and at the same time in some way to see yourself through their eyes.

The mirror tells the truth

We trust the mirror, don't we? But when we look in the mirror we make a mistake. In society in the third stage you look in the mirror and you say, 'I am that.' You imagine that face there is here. But you are wrong. Your face is not *here*, it's *there in the mirror*. You think you've got it right, you are absolutely sure you are right—'I am that one here.' But you are making a mistake.

Then when you enter the fourth stage of life you realise that your face is there and there's nothing here but Room for others. But you still play the game, you are still involved. In fact you can now play the game better because you're not hooked on the one-in-the-mirror in the same way, so you are not face-to-face with others and therefore are not confronting others, are not isolated from others. You are built Open. It's a whole different game. A completely different game. Society tells us that the game ended when we looked in the mirror and put that face on here at our Centre. It's like watching a film and getting to the end of it and thinking, 'Was that it?' Then you find the second DVD! 'Oh wow! That was not the end!' Stage four, the seer, is the second DVD. The 'headless way' is Season Two! It's fantastic. Everything is inside-out and upside-down from what we were told. Yet we continue playing the game. Fantastic.

You are like me

Now that you see you are not in a group, that all groups are in you,

you realise that, for anyone you meet, this must be true for them too. I can see Roger there but I know that you, Roger, from your point of view, are full of everybody else. This changes my view of others because, before I get the second DVD, I look at others and I act as if others are just their appearance. 'You are a solid thing over there, you are limited, you are separate from me—I am not you.' But when I get the second DVD I look and I think to myself, 'Alright, that is what you look like. But now, because you are like me, I know that you are also looking out of this Open Space. You are not a solid thing, you are Nothing-full-of-everything. You are not limited, you are infinite. You are not separate from me—I am you and you are me.' If I take this seriously, this must change how I behave towards 'others'.

Douglas Harding wrote about how seeing his Original Face affected him in his book *On Having No Head*. He said, more or less (I'm paraphrasing)—'I saw I was headless and there were two things I realised right away. The first was that I was face-to-No-face with others—I was built open for others. I confronted no one because I was 'face-to-face' with no one. My second realisation was that everyone must be in the same condition as I was. Everyone must be built open for others and the world.' Which led him then to 'think the world of' everyone.' When you 'think the world of someone', it means you have tremendous respect for them. But the respect that Douglas was thinking about was not based on what kind of person someone might be but rather on the fact that they were not a person at all, they were Room for the world. Right now I know that where Charlie is, at Charlie's Centre, isn't Charlie but the world. You are Capacity for the world. You are Space where you are just like I am. Saying 'I think the world of you' is not based on a well-meaning fantasy about others but on a realistic assessment of others. This is who others really are. I think the world of you because you are the world. Living in the light of this Reality our lives begin to open and open, to deepen and deepen. The second DVD never stops playing!

Chapter 18

Confidence

Richard: Seeing who you really are is direct experience. It is waking up to Reality. Now you have found a stable foundation to your life.

Dale: Absolute confidence. The only thing you can be sure of. Direct experience.

Charles: Having absolute confidence—isn't that egotistical? Thinking you know it all—isn't that an ego thing?

Richard: The confidence I'm referring to is not about being confident in yourself personally. I am not talking about me being confident in Richard, about being absolutely confident in him, I am talking about what I am inwardly, this Open Space which is full of everything. This is real. This is reliable. This never changes—the Whole, the Nothing that is always full of something is not in time. Every individual thing is in time, it's coming and going. This workshop is coming and going. But the One is outside time, it doesn't change. So you can be confident of it in the sense that it is always there, whether you like it or not.

There's also another sense in which I can be confident in the One—I am confident that the One is infinitely wise. It is wise because it is. It has happened. It knows how to Be, to emerge into Existence from the darkest of all nights, the darkness of non-being. That emergence, that explosion into Being is a miracle. That is clever. Your True Self is supremely clever! I am sure of that.

We distinguish between ourselves personally and the One, between the individual things within the One that come and go and are not absolutely reliable, and the One itself which never comes or goes. If you can't trust the One who neither comes nor goes, who has achieved Being—who is achieving Being right now—what can you trust?

Chapter 19

The Tube

The Tube experiment focuses attention on the obvious fact that when you look at someone else you see their face and not your own. We call it being 'face-to-No-face'. We also call it 'trading faces'. I've got your face now and you've got mine. This is the opposite of what others see, isn't it? When I look at you, Anne, others see our two faces—yours is there and mine is here. But for us it's the opposite—we *trade* faces. Being aware of this, any face now potentially becomes a reminder of your No-face. Seeing anyone's face can now remind you that you don't have one. Whenever you are with someone you are receiving their face in your Space. It's a loving thing to do. The Tube experiment focuses our attention on this—on being Space-to-face with others.

A couple of years ago I decided to do the Tube near the beginning of a workshop. There was a woman sitting on my left who hadn't done a workshop before. I thought, 'Well, I will demonstrate the Tube with her. Why not?' She was up for it, so we looked in the Tube to show the rest of the group what to do. When she came out she exclaimed, 'Oh my God, I just became a man!'

You become the other!

Find someone to do the Tube experiment with.

When you look through the Tube at the other person you don't have to look at them in the eyes. You can if you want but it's not primarily a communication exercise. If you want to communicate, smile or whatever, of course you can. I'm just clarifying the basic purpose of the experiment which is to notice what it's like at your end of the Tube and how your end contrasts with the far end. If you feel a bit self-conscious in the Tube, that's normal.

Look in the Tube with your partner.

You see a face at the far end—do you see a face at your end?

Isn't the set-up face there at the far end to no face here at the near end?

You are not face-to-face with the person there but face there to No-face here. Is that true?

Aren't you built Open at the near end—Capacity for the face at the far end?

Come out, close your eyes for a moment and rest.

Okay, open your eyes and look in again.

Whose face do you have now?

Having no face of your own, couldn't you say that the other person's face is yours?

Might you not even say, 'Being empty here, I am Room for you. I am you.'

This is a non-verbal experience, so if my words don't fit for you, choose your own, or don't use any words at all.

Come out, close your eyes and rest.

Open your eyes. Any reactions to share?

Brian: I have got her face.

Richard: It's good isn't it? Now, looking at me, you have my face!

Brian: This was incredible for me because up till now I've been doing it on my own at home with the mirror. I take the Tube to the mirror and my face is there at the far end. I find it a very profound experience. What was interesting about this experience is I felt I was becoming the other face. It was my face.

Richard: Isn't that beautiful!

Angela: I felt that with John. I was taking on his face.

Kevin: I thought I had someone else's head on my shoulders.

Richard: Yes, isn't it incredible? It's astonishing, wonderful. What a joy to become the other person.

David: It feels vulnerable. You are aware of your own face, that you are ageing.

Eric: Face-to-No-face—from the evidence of your own experience there's no ageing on your side of the Tube.

Brian: On the second go the other face became my face. That switch was startling.

Carol: This experiment made the Emptiness seem so alive. The face there in the Emptiness here.

Richard: Laurens van der Post wrote a book about the Kalahari bushmen. When he was with one of the bushmen they saw another bushman in the distance, running towards them with a spear. He came right up to them, stuck his spear into the sand and said the Kalahari greeting—'I was dead, now I am alive.' This Emptiness is dead without what fills it.

Margaret: At the near end of the Tube is the Nothingness, that Capacity for everything. Then something arises there. You are dead until you have some connection like that but it is not happening to a face. The fact it's happening where there isn't a face is an incredible experience.

Anne: I could see that this end was completely open and Gloria was there. Gloria was the only thing there. I was nothing, she was there.

George: From a distance, if we stared at each other for a while, I would feel self-conscious.

Richard: Yes, you would.

George: But I didn't in the Tube because I wasn't there.

Richard: You see the potential benefit of this! This is deep therapy, isn't it?

George: Yes.

Nigel: I was thinking, 'What does he think I look like?' Then I thought, 'That's just a thought!'

Richard: Yes, it is. And that thought did not obscure your No-face, did it?

Nigel: It got in the way.

Richard: Did it? Think the thought that I can see you, now. Hold that thought for a moment. Are you feeling self-conscious?

Nigel: Yes.

Richard: While you are thinking it now, whilst you are feeling self-conscious, can you see your face?

Nigel: No.

Richard: So it doesn't get in the way, does it?

Nigel: No.

Richard: No.

Nigel: It does and it doesn't.

Richard: No, I'm not going to let you off that one. How does it stop you seeing your No-face, if you choose to see it?

Nigel: Right, it's a choice.

Richard: It's a choice, isn't it? Yes. And you are free to make that choice no matter what is going on. Is that true?

Nigel: Yes.

Richard: That's how it is for me.

Nigel: I just have to remember, over and over and over.

Dale: As a traditional Buddhist practitioner, that experience magnified my fundamental practice. The words, 'I am Capacity for you'—they ring true from my experience. It is wide-open. This experiment allows me to have a deepening of that Openness. I notice that when thoughts occur, there isn't any place that they can stick to on this side of the Tube. It's just wide-open. If I pay attention to the thought, then I experience the thought, but if I pay attention to the Openness, the thought is like a cloud in the sky of my experience. There's no place for the thought to stick to. That's why it doesn't matter whether I like the thought or not, there is no place for that thought to stick to. That's unconditional freedom.

Richard: Wonderful. Thank you.

Steve: I remember when I first did this experiment. When I met the other person's gaze it was as if they were seeing right through me. Seeing through the little me, my appearance—seeing into my shame, all those layers that even I am not willing to look at. So I try to abide as the headless Space in the midst of all that shame, so all those layers can come in.

Richard: Beautiful. I understand. You are safe as that headless Space, aren't you?

Steve: Yes.

Jennifer: A total lack of confrontation. There wasn't a 'me' looking at my partner. In my experience there was simply my partner. No pressure, no self-consciousness, just this Field and there's my partner in it, in the Field of Awareness. Simple. Very simple.

Laura: A sense of merging.

Mark: It's one thing if you're relating as that empty Space to somebody else who is being a thing because you can be the empty Space and they are being that thing. But if two people are being No-thing the whole thing goes flat. Two No-things being Nothing together has a different quality.

Richard: Yes and no—because no one else loses their head.

Mark: From my point of view?

Richard: Yes.

Mark: You still have your head, for me.

Richard: Yes. Everyone else keeps their head. And everyone is aware of their own head.

Mark: But I sense that you don't have a head.

Richard: I know! That's why I said yes and no. This is the beauty of it—it's both/and. Everyone is aware both of their head and their No-head. This is the One become Many.

Mark: I guess what I'm saying is that something happens to the game in that moment of Seeing.

Richard: It does.

Margaret: It stops being the game. That's a beautiful thing.

Richard: It's a different game. You don't stop playing the game but it's a different game. Up to the point before you see who you are, you see people only as things. Very nice things but they are objects. When you see who you really are, you also see who others really are—although the only Space you see is where you are, it goes right around the other side of others and through them, doesn't it?

Margaret: Yes.

Richard: You can't contain who you really are. So you are now seeing that the other person is both a thing, and isn't.

Mark: Isn't?

Richard: There's only one Space that goes all the way around and includes the other. The Space belongs as much to the other person as it does to you. It's the One talking to itself.

Mark: Right.

Richard: Being both two and one. What a wonderful thing.

Eric: I'm still in the stage where I want to jump back into the game sometimes.

Richard: Yes. You're not doing it wrong. You can't do it wrong. That urge to jump into the game is what got the game going in the first place. I think you've got to keep doing that. There's nothing wrong with that because you can have the urge to jump back in the game while you're seeing the Space. So that's okay too. And it's very good to forget who you are sometimes because then when you remember, you have a beautiful surprise.

Chapter 20
Two-Way Communication

This experiment involves communicating the truth of who you are in public. They say, if you want to learn, teach. Or you could say, if you want to learn, communicate. If you want to learn, go public! You'll learn a lot if you go public!

When you share with another person something that is true for you, it's not more true after you've shared it than it was before you shared it, but in some way it's more real. It's now out there in the public domain. Now other people know about it. When others hear it and reflect it back to you, something changes. Not only is this true when we talk about ourselves personally, this is also the case when we express the reality of who we really are. In this experiment I'm going to invite you to talk about who you really are in public—in this group—communicating to others your experience of your True Self. I'm not talking about anything complicated, simply about describing being headless.

Normally when we communicate with someone we talk not only about ourselves but about the other person as well. If I'm in conversation with Chris here, I'll tell Chris about myself and Chris will tell me about himself. But I'll also reflect back my impression of him in some way or other and he will do the same for me. In that way we get to see ourselves through the other's eyes. So we are not just thinking about ourselves, we are also thinking and feeling for the other person. We put ourselves in their shoes. It's a two-way exchange. In this experiment we are going to explore communicating in this way with our True Identity as the focus.

Instructions

I will demonstrate with Chris how you do this. Since there are two sides to this exercise, one of you will be A and the other B. I'm A and Chris, you're B. Since I'm A, I'll start. First I'm going to describe my True Nature to Chris. Then I'm going to put myself in B's shoes — Chris' shoes — and describe his experience. Then B has a go. You'll see what I mean.

I'm speaking from my point of view first — Chris, I am built Open for you. I have your face instead of my own. I see your face there given in my Space here. I am Room for you. I am looking out of a Single Eye here. I am wide-open and in this Openness I find all my sensations, thoughts, and you.

Do you see what I'm doing? I am communicating to another person who I am. I am saying this directly to Chris, directly to this person here, not abstractly into the air to nobody in particular. Chris, I have your face right here where I am. I am empty for you.

Now I'm going to put myself in Chris' shoes and describe how it is from his point of view. Just a few sentences is enough. From your point of view Chris, you don't see Chris' face there — you are built Open for Richard, for me. You are Empty there where you are. (I can use gestures, using my hands to bring Chris' attention to his Space there.) You are wide-Open there, your Eye is Single, you include everything. All of your experience is floating in the Nothingness there. You are Space now for me. You are totally Still there.

Now it's your turn Chris. So first you describe your side.

Chris: Richard, I am built Open for you. I am Space for your face. I am completely wide-open, like a mirror.

Richard: Fantastic. Now place yourself in my position.

Chris: Richard, you are built Open for me. You are Space, you are No-thing full of Chris.

Richard: Thank you. Perfect. Okay, decide who is A and who is B. The idea is to help each other be aware of who you both really are. When you place yourself in the other person's position, simply describe their View.

Feeling seen as who you are

When someone is describing to you what it's like to be who you really are, notice what it's like to receive their communication. I'll do this experiment now with John. I'm going to put myself in your shoes, John, and imagine what it's like to be you now. I want you to check out whether or not you feel seen as who you really are. Alright?

So, I'm placing myself in your position. You are headless there, you are wide-open, you have no boundary, you are immense there, you go on for ever, there is just one View there. At the moment your View is filled not only with Richard but also with all your sensations and with all the sounds going on in the Space.

Do you feel seen as who you really are?

John: It's amazing. It's fantastic. I've got to tell you, it's absolutely wonderful. Really, that's profound. You just opened me up. It was great. You were describing my True Nature and seeing that True Nature as my potential. You are just laying it on for me. You were giving me the truth. And you presented it as a fact which makes it really hard to say no to. That's really beautiful. Thank you very much.

Taking empathy a step further

Peter: I get that, the power of putting it out there. But if I'm out on the street with you, having a cup of tea or something and I hardly know you, why am I telling you that you are headless?

Richard: You are already telling people who they are at the human level. If we met on the street you wouldn't just talk about you, you would be putting yourself in my shoes, at least to some degree, and you would think and feel for me to some degree. Even if you tell me I'm looking well or I'm looking tired, you are in some way placing yourself in my position and feeling for me. So we are already doing that. We are already moving back and forth between our own point of view and the other's point of view. When you empathise with another, you are seeing things from their point of view. Normally we are empathising with one another at the human level and when someone empathises with you accurately, you feel seen and understood and hopefully appreciated. It's a good thing to do. It affects the way you feel about yourself. Most of us are pretty good at doing that. In this exercise we are taking that empathy one step further. In other words I'm not just empathising with what it's like to be you in terms of what you think and feel and so on, I am also empathising with you in terms of you being Space for the world. You are Capacity for the world, including being Capacity for what you think and feel. Normally we don't talk about this side of another person. When we do, we are reflecting back who they really are.

Peter: But the other person might not want to listen.

Richard: Yes, but we are in a group where people do want to listen.

Dale: What I was hearing was that you were thinking it was about going up to a stranger and talking about it.

Richard: No, I wouldn't suggest that.

Dale: It's good that you clarify that.

Richard: I'm not suggesting that. Clearly the other person has to be interested. It's no good imposing this on others. But let's say I am the other person and you know I am interested. You have talked about your experience of being headless. Once you have told me about who you really are, you are free to say, 'By the way, you are the same as me. You are also built Open for the world.' In other words, you don't stop at just telling me who *you* really are, you also go on to reflect that I am this Space too. In this room we are amongst friends so it's okay to do this. Everyone here has come to experience who they really are. So I'm free to say to you, 'You also are built Open. You also are Space for others.' This is a deep and beautiful thing to tell someone. Why stop short at their humanity? Why only exchange views about who we are as people when you also know about who you really are? This is an invitation to communicate about who we really are as well as about our humanity. Of course I'm not saying you should. Feel your way with what is appropriate. When you look at me — you can do it with me now — you are headless and you are room for Richard. Is that True?

Peter: Yes. But the idea that this boundless scene that is right in front of me, is me — that's the part I'm trying to work out.

Richard: I don't think we'll ever understand it, but we can bathe in it.

Peter: Okay, I like that. And you, like me, are headless. You have me as part of your Space. And I am in your head! In your No-head!

Richard: I am in you, you are in me. I am you and you are me.

Roger: I am one hundred per cent sure about this in terms of my own experience, but when I say that you are the same, that you are headless there... I am experiencing this directly here where I am but I am not experiencing it directly over there where you are. I am assuming you are the Space. Perhaps I could say I'm ninety-nine per cent certain you are the Space, as you were saying before.

Richard: I'm headless for you, and I'm ninety-nine per cent certain that you are headless for me — I understand that. But now think about it in terms of listening — as I'm looking at you, I am listening to myself speaking. I can't see my mouth so for me my voice is not coming out of my mouth here but out of the Nothing. My words are appearing in the Silence here. When you speak your voice also arises in the same Silence. It's sort of over there and it's Roger's voice, and Richard's voice is over here and it's Richard's, but both voices are happening in this One Consciousness. I am this One Consciousness so I am speaking with two voices. I am absolutely sure that our two voices are in one Consciousness. Is that true for you?

Roger: Yes, I experience it here.

Richard: Yes, it's all here in one Consciousness, isn't it?

Roger: Yes.

Richard: Anyone else want to try this? 'I am headless, I am room for you. You are headless, you are room for me.' You can improvise on that theme.

George: I am open Space for you, for your face, for your appearance. And you are open Awareness, open Space for my appearance.

Namaste

Richard: This is a deep way of appreciating others. You are not only appreciating them as things — I am now also appreciating you as Room for everybody else. This is bringing this Reality onto the front burner. Everyone here is Space for everyone else. This is recognising who we all really are. This is recognising that I am you and you are me. When Indian people greet each other with the 'namaste' gesture, putting their palms together when they meet someone, what that means is—'I honour the One in you. The One there in you is the same One as the One here in me. We two are One.' This is what we're doing here—I am acknowledging and honouring the fact that what I am here is Room for you, and what you are there is Room for me. The one who is Room for others is the One. Acknowledging this is truly respecting yourself and others. I can't see how you can give anyone higher respect and recognition than recognising who they really are. This is the truth about us. Society has not yet woken up to this truth. This is not dreaming, this is not wishful thinking, it's not joining a club that believes in being the One—every way you test it, you are the One and everyone is the One. Whether you like it or not, it's true. And it's a fantastic truth. It's the best news in the world. You don't need it confirmed by anyone else, you see it for yourself.

Seeing who you really are is a healing thing. It is healing for yourself, but you cannot separate your healing from anyone you are with. When you are aware of your True Self you are being aware of it *for others* and *as others* because you cannot see who you really are without including others. Everyone is within you. You are Seeing not as a person but as the One—the One who is everybody. You are Seeing as and for everyone. When you see who you really are, you are the One who is within all beings waking up to yourself.

Like a wedding vow

I gave a workshop at a conference in California last year. We did this process whilst sitting in a circle rather than dividing off into pairs. One person would pick someone else in the circle and would do this exercise with them—'I am room for you and you are room for me', and so on. At the end of the workshop a man came up to me to talk. He was a Buddhist minister. He told me that watching people speak to each other like this had really moved him—doing it in the circle means that everyone witnesses the two people when they are speaking to each other. So everyone is involved, watching what is happening—watching two people communicate with each other about who they really are. The minister said that when people were doing this he felt they were blessing each other. I understood what he meant—it does feel like a blessing. When I say to you, 'You are wide-open now, you are Room for me and everything', this is the deepest blessing. When someone is speaking to you about your Openness, pointing to it, celebrating it, don't you feel deeply seen as who you really are? 'You are transparent there! You are wide-open there!' It's beautiful to be seen in this way, isn't it? You are being blessed.

He also said, 'As a minister I marry people, and listening to people speaking to each other like this was like hearing them making their wedding vows to each other!' I could see what he meant. This is the deepest declaration you can make to another person—'I am you and you are me.' It's like a wedding vow because you are declaring in public your profound connection with someone—your identity with someone.

I did this process with a group in Dublin earlier this year. It was a group in a training programme for lay people in a Catholic college. The group was meeting regularly so they knew each other well. I was invited to join them for a morning to share the experiments with them. I told them the story about the Buddhist minister and what he'd said about this exchange being like making a wedding vow. Then we began the experiment. A couple of people said they would go first—George and Linda. George said he would start—Linda was sitting across the circle from him. So George looked across at Linda (they were friends) and said, 'Linda, I am Room for you, I am Space for you, I am absolutely wide-open for you. I am you now. And you are me, you are Room for me, you are Space for me.' And Linda replied, 'I do, I do!' She had picked up on the wedding vow idea. It was very funny.

Non-verbal communication

The transmission of your state of consciousness is to a large degree non-verbal, whether you are in the stage of the baby, the child, the adult or the seer, so bringing non-verbal gestures into sharing Seeing can be effective. I'm moving my hands like this [in and out of my Void] and you know what I'm referring to — now that you have done some of the experiments. Now watch — I'm moving my hands apart in front of my face as if I'm opening curtains. Finally my hands disappear into the Space here, from my point of view. Try that. Does that work for you? It's opening and cleansing, isn't it?

Brendon: It doesn't work for me.

Richard: I'll do it with you. Look ahead, not particularly at me. I'm going to move my hands apart in front of your face as if I'm opening curtains in front of you, and then I'll move them into your Void, so that your attention is drawn to the open Space where you are.

Brendon: Oh yes!

Richard: In the workshop in California where we were honouring each other in this way, communicating to one another the reality of who we all really are, a woman said she wanted to do this exercise but non-verbally. She said she was a very verbal person, that she used words a lot, and she wanted to see if she could communicate her True Nature to someone and reflect back that person's True Nature without words. She looked across the circle at someone and made gestures to indicate she was headless, that she was Capacity for that other person, and then made gestures to indicate the other person was also Capacity, that the other person was Space for her. Then the other person did the same back to her, non-verbally. It was very effective and moving. We all knew exactly what the communication was about.

Non-visual senses

We can include the other senses in this way of communicating. I will show you with Steve. Steve, I am wide-open Space for you. Not only am I seeing that it is empty here for you and I have your face instead of my own, but my body sensations are floating around in this Space, they are at large, merging with the walls of the room.

Now I'm going to place myself in your position. There Steve, you don't see your face. You are wide-open, boundless, and you are full of Richard and everything else going on. But also, your body sensations are at large, they are floating in the Space there. Do you want to try it with me? Do your side, then my side.

Steve: I am noticing that I am headless. Richard is in my Space here. I also notice everything that is going on in the Space — my sensations, my feelings, what I hear and everything is all in the same Awareness as your head. And from your point of view, you are headless. You are Capacity for me, for sensations and sounds.

Richard: Thank you. When I do that to you, when I say that I am going to place myself in your position, Steve, and you are wide-open there, looking out of a Single Eye, and the Space there is full of thoughts and feelings and sensations and memories and things going on in the Space, don't you feel seen as who you really are?

Steve: Yes.

Margaret: This is wonderful that this is going on in this room. You have been pushing us to acknowledge and share things. All the sounds are coming from that one Space, multiple voices but One Consciousness. It's all there — everyone is experiencing their sensations in that One Space.

Richard: It's true, isn't it? We are built open for each other, for the world, for the stars.

Speaking for everyone

In another workshop there was a guy who arrived about an hour late to the workshop. Anyway we got him on board in about five minutes in terms of seeing who he really was. Then towards the end of the workshop we were doing this experiment — pick someone and communicate with them about being headless. He said, 'I would like to try it.' I said, 'Great!' Then he said, 'I don't want to do this exercise with just one person, I want to do it with you all.' My first thought was, 'Oh, that's not how you are meant to do it! You are meant to do it with just one person.' Then I thought, 'Just relax and see what happens.' First he said to the whole group, 'I am headless for all of you, you are all in me.' Then he said, 'And you are all headless for me.' He spoke for everyone. Then everyone in the group replied — 'We are headless for you and you are headless for us.' It was inspiring. It articulated the fact that when you find out who you really are you find out who everyone really is. Then you can speak for everyone. 'We are all Room for each other.' This is a profoundly different way of relating, isn't it? This is no longer just seeing ourselves as separate from each other. Your separate self is real. I respect that reality. I know we are separate in the sense that I know you don't experience my thoughts and feelings. All that is true. But this is also true — 'I am Room for you and you are Room for me. I am in you and you are in me.' Am I going to ignore that aspect of our relationship? Am I going to ignore the fact that you are in me and I am in you? I hope not!

Not a peak experience

Steve: I was affected and thrown off by what you did with John a while back because John's response was 'Wow! This is really incredible, something amazing has just happened.' I was waiting for something amazing to happen to me. But I think listening to everyone has helped resolve that.

Richard: What in the conversation since has resolved it for you?

Steve: Hearing about the different experiences of other people, the variety of responses, has helped me feel reassured that I don't have to get anything, that it's just acknowledging that this is the way it is. I have no problem acknowledging that but I was waiting to be enlightened!

Richard: It sounds like you are now distinguishing between the plain experience of who you really are and each person's different reaction to it. Brilliant. It's a learning curve for us all. We tend to think — 'That person has got it and I don't.' No! They are just having their experience which is different from yours. Their experience will change. John, your experience, your reaction, has now changed, hasn't it? Right now are your feelings different from what they were when we had that interaction?

John: Yes, they have changed. A little bit.

Dale: That's why we make a distinction in our Zen tradition between what the by-products are — the by-products can be exhilarating or fearful. They go in many directions. I like the term 'unconditioned presence' — it's emphasising more the neutral side of that. Those experiences whether they are elation or they are fear are always arising in that same open empty Space which sees them equally. There is the impartiality and equality of it all, the composure, the peace, the equanimity right there as a natural reality. It can allow for the full expression of it to go in any direction, to expand or contract. When people have peak experiences, all of a sudden that's happening, but then surely they wake up tomorrow and they've lost it. You can't lose this.

John: Yes, I am elated now, but I don't know how else to be.

Richard: It's alright to feel elated!

Dale: We are just making a distinction between that which comes and goes, the sensations, and the actual Reality.

Richard: The experience is non-verbal so there are many different ways of thinking about it and reacting to it. As you go on with this neutral, non-verbal experience, different ways of understanding it will unfold. It won't all come today. And what comes today will go. But what remains is the neutral experience. It's as if you keep going up in a balloon and then coming down to the ground. The ground is always there but your realisations and feelings are always changing. Before you might have thought, 'Oh great, I'm at the top of the balloon ride and being at the top is Reality.' But then you come down so you think you're no longer experiencing Reality. But no, Reality is the ground that is always there, underneath your feelings which are always going up and down. You continue to have these waves of understanding and feeling and openness, but now you are aware of the neutral experience underlying these changing states of mind — this neutral Reality which you have access to anytime, at will. If Reality was being at the top of the balloon ride then you wouldn't have access to it at will, but because it is the ground underneath everything, the Ground of Being, this plain Nothingness that is always available no matter what you are feeling—you cannot see your head—you can access it at will. It is neutral, free, the same for all.

Andrew: You can't be Space for their Space—there's just one Space.

Richard: A good way of putting it.

Andrew: I'm asking...

Richard: I'm not going to tell you because you don't need me to tell you. I'm just saying it's interesting for me to hear you describe it in that way. It opens up another way of thinking about things.

Chapter 21

A Creation Story

Our development through the four stages of the baby, the child, the adult and the seer can be told as a kind of creation myth, a story. Here is my version of this story—

In the beginning was the One. The One is you—you only experience one Single Eye, which is yours. Only one View, only one field of sensation, only one field of thinking. You are the One—this story is about you.

In the beginning was the One.

Before the beginning there was nothing. You can't imagine that because if you imagine nothing then you're there imagining it, so there's no longer nothing. But this is a story and in a story you can imagine the impossible. So before the beginning there was nothing—an endless dark night of non-being.

Bang! You happen!

Then, Bang! You happen. God happens. Picture God in some way. I'm going to picture an old man with a beard (I know, I'm conventional!) but please come up with your own image. It's a story. So one moment there's nothing and the next moment there's God, appearing miraculously out of nothing—out of less than nothing.

You can imagine God feeling absolutely bowled over. 'Where did I come from? I have just appeared out of nothing, out of nowhere! How did I do that?' I have achieved Being! That's impossible! Pure magic!'

You are the One. This is a story about *you*. This is *your* astonishment at *your* existence, *your* self-creation. 'This is amazing. I can't explain myself. I am! How amazing to Be. I don't know how I came to Be but I did. I just conceived myself! No one else has done this. I alone have achieved Being!'

You are in shock. You can't get over the astonishing fact you've happened—without help, without planning, without anything! You pinch yourself to make sure you're not dreaming...

Your existence is a surprise and a mystery to you.

You say to yourself, 'That was clever! In fact, that was brilliant! Pure genius! I just invented myself out of nothing!'

Your next thought is, 'This is so good, I would love to share this with someone.'

If something good happens to you it's natural to want to share it. Say you get a new job or you win a prize—when you share your good news something changes because the person you share it with can reflect it back to you in their own words, so you get to see it in a different way. Your understanding grows. And they can celebrate with you, so your joy grows.

Achieving Being is the most amazing Good News, so it's natural to want to share it. 'This is brilliant to Be. I would love to share my excitement about Being with someone.'

But of course there's no one to share it with because you're the only one who is! You are the Alone, the Incomparable One, the 'one without a second'. You alone have achieved Being.

You feel frustrated you cannot share your joy. You also feel lonely. (It's a story!)

'How good it would be to have a friend with whom I can share my wonder, my excitement, my joy!'

You are also bored. 'I would love to go on an adventure, to go travelling, but there's nowhere to go—there's nothing outside Me, nowhere apart from here. If there were other places then I could go away, see new things, take a few risks and experience the thrill of adventure. I like the safety of Being but I would also like to feel the thrill of adventure.'

Nowhere to go and nothing to do—just Being, Being, Being. It's always the same. No change, no time, no past to look back on, no future to look forward to, no 'others' to go on adventures with to 'other places'.

Stage One — The Baby

This is a story! It's a story about you — about who you really are. The beginning of the story relates to the beginning of your life. When you were a baby you did not yet know about 'others' — you had no developed idea of other minds. Nor had you yet developed the idea of other places. Your world was only what was physically given in your Eye and no more. Nor had you developed the idea of time — the past and the future had not yet occurred to you. There was only now. Simply put, there was only one Consciousness, only here, and only now. In stage one you were that One I am talking about in this story — the One without another, without other places, without other times.

In this first stage you as the One don't really know yourself because you have nothing to compare yourself with. As a baby, not only do you not know either about yourself as a person or about others, you have no idea about the One. You are the One without knowing you are the One. Of course without language you can't even think about any of this.

In this story you come up with a solution to your lack of friends and adventure and your ignorance about who you really are. Your response is to create self and others, space and time — so that you have others to share your joy with, and so that there are places to travel to and the time in which to do such things. And the ability to go away will mean you can then return and know yourself in a new way. How can you create all this out of nothing? It sounds impossible. You haven't a clue how to do it. But you realise that as the One you have already achieved one impossible thing before breakfast — Being! Two impossible things are no more impossible than one. So you create self, others, space and time.

Stage Two — The Child

But to begin with self and others are not real. They are like cardboard cut-outs, just 'pictures-in-consciousness'. They have no independent reality. Because they are not real they don't satisfy your need to relate—from a real person here to real others there. This stage in the story corresponds to the second stage of the infant or child when you are beginning to learn that you are the one-in-the-mirror, that there are others, that there's a world that's separate from you and there's time, but you haven't yet really taken all that on board as reality. You want a real self, and others to go on adventures with, but at this stage—in the story!—self and others are no more real than characters in a computer game. If you lose your 'avatar', your 'hero' in the game, or one of your friends, it doesn't make any difference because it's not real. It's like watching a film but being aware you're a spectator, so you're not really involved. You don't feel that what happens in the film is real. In a computer game you can jump in front of a bus for fun because you know you can't die. But after a while, where's the fun in that? You remember the game of stickers we played? If you treat it as 'just a game' you don't really care what happens. It doesn't matter if you're right or wrong about yourself or others because 'it's just a game.' But as some of us found, if we do identify with the sticker, the game is not just a game. We care about what happens.

In this story you realise that in order for others and the world to be real and convincing and poignant and true, you've got to forget you're God and become one of the characters—in the film, in the story, in life. Forgetting you are God and identifying with your appearance means you'll take yourself as a person seriously and therefore take others seriously as well.

At this point in the story, before you become fully identified with the one-in-the-mirror, you pause. You wonder, 'Is there any guarantee I will remember I'm God further down the line?' You realise there's no guarantee. Perhaps you will never remember. Nervous about what might happen, you step back from becoming a person. This corresponds to the moments in childhood when you regress to being a baby again. It's safer to be the One, dreaming in the bubble of Oneness, so you withdraw from the 'real world', from 'real others', from all responsibility for your 'self'.

But before long—in the story!—you as God realise you don't want to stay wrapped up in your cocoon, in the predictable safety and aloneness of the One. You want adventure, you want company. You realise the only way forward is to forget you are God and become a person in a world of real others, taking the risk that you may never remember who you really are.

I've forgotten the exact details of the scene in the film *The Matrix*, but I think Morpheus gives the hero Neo a choice—if he takes the blue pill then he stays in the Matrix, in the dream, but if he takes the red pill he wakes up to reality. When you are in the Matrix you don't know you're dreaming, you think it's reality. Something like that anyway. In this creation story, becoming a person is the moment of going into the dream. If you choose to become a person and forget you are God, you forget you have chosen. You forget it's not 'real'.

So it's a scary decision to make. But after hovering on the brink for a while you decide it's worth the risk because you don't want to go on feeling lonely and bored. (It's a story!). You think: 'I'm going to take the risk of forgetting I'm God and becoming a person in this incredible game I've created, the game of life. I know that if I become a person then this game will no longer be a game because it will be the only game, the only story. It will be real. But I'm going to take the risk and jump into being a person.'

You jump.

We all made that choice. It's not a conscious choice but we all made it. We all jumped. We all became the one-in-the-mirror.

Stage Three—The Adult

In the third stage you are God unaware you are God. You are God fully convinced you are a person in society. You don't treat yourself like a computer game character that you can throw in front of a bus for fun. You are real. What happens to you and to others matters. You can no longer be a train or a bird or a monster, you are now a person. In this stage the idea of being anything other than a person is a delusion, and the idea of being God is not just stupid and mad, it's also blasphemous. You are a human being who was born and will die. That's who you are. You are now profoundly unaware of your True Self. This stage is reflected in those fairy stories where the hero or heroine is under a spell. In adulthood we are bewitched, spell-bound, under the profound delusion that we are what we look like. God is looking in the mirror and is convinced he is that one there, that he is inside that body and that others are separate beings just like he is. You are looking in the mirror and you are convinced you are that appearance. You have no idea that the one looking is God — that you who are looking are God.

As we grew up we learned that the world and time and others have always been there — we were simply not yet aware of them. But my experience is that in the beginning of my life they were not there. Over a period of months and years these things emerged in my Consciousness — the Many arose out of the One, out of Me. I as the One flowered into the Many. I as the One created self and others, the world and time. Then during adulthood I denied that I did so! I disowned my creation. I hoodwinked myself!

Most of us think this third stage is the end of the story. Society tells us that this is what life is all about — growing up is about finding out who you are in society, taking responsibility more or less for being that one (when convenient!), and making the best of the cards you were dealt. At some point you might think, 'Is this really all there is to life? I've found out who I am as a person — is this it? Is this as good as it gets?'

But there's a fourth stage — which is hidden from us in the third stage. The fourth stage is re-awakening to who we really are. If you're lucky you hear about this fourth stage. You come across the rumour that there's more to you than you'd been told, that you are not just the one-in-the-mirror. In this workshop you are testing this rumour. From the point of view of who you really are, you are God deciding to take a fresh look at yourself. Aware you might have made a mistake about what you are, you decide to question the way you see yourself, the way society tells you to see yourself.

Stage Four — The Seer

I said that you took the risk that you might never re-discover who you really are. It seemed that way. In fact you discover now that you left some clues about your True Nature scattered around.

William: Breadcrumbs.

Richard: Yes. Here's one clue, one signpost you left lying about — point again at where others see your face. Luckily you put this reminder in place so you could see your True Self today. You were kind to yourself. But now that you are aware of being the One, do you forget about being a person? No. Do you now revert to treating others as just 'pictures–in–consciousness'? No. You are the One, yet at the same time you think and feel and act with every fibre of your being as if you as a person are real and others are real.

Now you have got what you originally wanted because in the beginning you wanted real friends with whom you could share your excitement and your joy about Being, and with whom you could go on adventures. Here we are. Here in this workshop are real others with whom you are spending the day exploring what it's like to be the One. These others are reflecting on being the One in all kinds of ways you would never think of on your own. How brilliant is that! To awaken to the One but have everyone agreeing about it would be a pointless exercise, wouldn't it? You didn't set up this incredible world just to get everyone saying the same thing. No. You wanted as wide a range of reactions as possible. Here we are — everyone is different, everyone is expressing being the One in their own way.

Originally — in the story — you were bored, you wanted to go on adventures. Having an adventure means you have to have somewhere to go. Although you cannot see it at the moment, you accept there's a room on the other side of that door. And though you only hear that dog barking and don't see it, you accept it's not just a sound — there's a real dog there. We accept the independent existence of the world and of others which means there are real places we can go to with real others. And we accept the reality of time which we didn't know about in the first stage of the baby, so we can plan to do things in the future and look back on our past experience. But for adventure to be real there needs to be an element of danger, of risk, of uncertainly and not-knowing—if you know exactly what's going to happen and there's no risk at all, it's not an adventure. It's something else—called 'boring'! But life is not completely predictable or safe. As the One you have set up this amazing situation that contains risk and danger and is full of surprises. Even with the simplest things you don't know exactly what's going to happen next. I've just raised my hand—did anyone know I was going to do that? I didn't!

These things are what we wanted at the beginning of the story. We wanted others who are really 'other', who are not in our control. Wouldn't it be lovely if everyone did just what I wanted? No! It would be good only for about five minutes! Wouldn't it be wonderful if there was no risk at all in my life? No. For five minutes only. There's no adventure without risk.

So today we are exploring this fourth stage, the stage of being the One *and* being a person. Now I can look at Eric and have a conversation with him about who we both really are. I can say, 'I am the One, I have happened, how brilliant! Isn't it amazing to be the One?'

Eric: It's a mystery.

Richard: It's a mystery, yes. I know what you mean!

If something has happened to you and you share it with someone else who has had a similar experience, you know they will understand better than someone who has not had that experience. So really, you as the One want to meet others who are also the One—impossible though it would seem to be—because they will know what it's like to be the One. They will know what it's like to Be. So Laurie, I'm the One and I've happened. I AM! Do you know what I mean? Do you too know what it's like to Be?

Laurie: Yes! I know the edges of it.

Richard: I know the edges of it! What a great way of putting it. Isn't talking to others about being the One a wonderful paradox?

The One is many so it can talk to itself about being One and many! That's brilliant. So, well done for being the One! The Only One! I congratulate you on achieving Being!

The feeling of separation, of self and others, is not a mistake we should try and get rid of when we see who we really are. It is what we wanted all along. We wanted to be both One and many. Why would we choose to revert to being just the One-without-others when we can be the One *and* have others? We can have our cake and eat it! We can be both totally safe as who we really are and experience the thrill of adventure, of danger, of risk.

David: I am there. I have never heard anyone telling my story before.

Richard: This story is your life story. The transformation of the One into the One-that-is-many happened within your life-time. When you were new-born you were the One without knowing about others. It wasn't so very long ago. In the few years of your life you have been on this incredible journey of forgetting, of going away from who you really are. Now when you re-awaken to being the One and to the fact that everything comes out of you, you can say, 'This is what I wanted. I wanted others so I could share the joy of Being with them. My dream came true. My dream is coming true now. Amazing.'

Chapter 22

The Great Storehouse

Please find your way into groups of three. One person sits down on a chair—I'll call them A. A is going to experience being the Storehouse. Then B stands in front of A and C stands behind A. C is holding a small collection of objects.

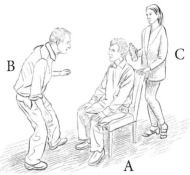

A—simply look ahead. This is not a communication exercise. I'm going to demonstrate what you do in this experiment. I'll act as B—I stand in front of A.

I'm not looking in A's eyes—I'm not communicating with A. I'm aware that A is looking out of Open Space. We are going to call that Space 'the Great Storehouse'. The Storehouse is the place from which everything comes and to which everything returns. I'm looking at A but I'm pretending to look not at a person there but into the Space there, into the Storehouse, so that A can have the impression I'm looking into their Space.

Now I'm going to reach into A's Space with my hand. I'm putting my hand into A's Void—reaching into the Great Storehouse. Now I bring my hand back out. I'll do it again. Now my hand is disappearing into the Great Storehouse but this time I'm going to see what's in there. As I reach in this time, C who is standing behind A gives me one of the objects she is holding. So when I bring my hand out this time I bring that object out of the Space there, out of the Great Storehouse.

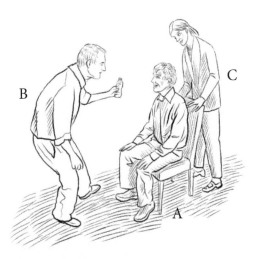

The experience that A has is that this object comes out of Nothing, out of the Storehouse. Something is coming out of Nothing! So, play with this. Each person has a go at being A, at being the Great Storehouse.

Okay, that's the experiment.

You could say that this whole workshop is coming out of the Great Storehouse! Magic! Everything is coming out of the Nothing all the time. Creation is happening all the time. Noticing this is living a life of magic, a life of wonder.

Chapter 23

The Well of Time

We'll do the two-way pointing gesture again.

With one hand you are pointing out into the room. It's now almost ten past three in the afternoon—we are looking there into a moment in time. We started the workshop at 10 o'clock this morning and now it's almost ten past three. At the same time as pointing into the room, into this moment in time, with your other hand you are pointing back into the Space—what time is it there?

Angela: Timeless.

Richard: Timeless. Just as it is face-to-No-face, so it is time-to-No-time. Change there to no change here. I don't see anything moving here—no change, no time.

Dale: Could I request the timeless circle?

Richard: Sure—The Well Of Time. To do this we need to stand in a No-head Circle.

Look down at your own body. Notice it's coming out of Nothing. Your body is headless, it's coming out of this Open Space above your chest.

Now be aware of the circle of feet, the circle of legs—all the bodies vanish at the top into one No-head. There are no dividing lines in this No-head. Down there we are many, at the top we are One.

Now we'll put a clock down there on the floor in the middle of the circle. Look at the clock. It's eleven minutes past three. The hands of the clock are moving round the face of the clock. They are marking out time. Time and change go together. Time is passing—the moving hands are marking out the passage of time.

As you are looking down at the clock, notice where your body is disappearing into—into this Space at the top. Can you see any change here? Any movement here? Where there's no movement there's no change, and where there's no change there's no time. You are looking from the Timeless here into time there.

You don't have to feel anything in particular—it's a neutral observation. You don't have to understand it in any particular way. There you see change—the hands are marking out time. And here at the top—no change, no time.

This circle is only going to last a minute or two. It is in time. It's a temporary home of yours. For a few minutes your home is this circle, but in a few moments this home will be gone. But at the top this Open Space will never go—this is your Eternal Home. You never leave this Home. Welcome Home!

Okay, we can sit down.

The circle has gone now but the Space is still present. Time there to no time here.

Chapter 24

Real Drama

Imagine you are watching a film, a thriller, and the relationship between the lead actors is going well... until something terrible happens and it all goes wrong. But then, in most films I suppose, it works out in the end. The problem is resolved. That's drama. It makes the film interesting. The tension is creative.

There's also drama in our lives, a moment when it seems that everything has gone wrong. In the beginning you were the One. Then you lost awareness of being the One. 'Oh no, it's all gone wrong! I'm in a body now, I'm trapped. Oh no! What's going to happen now? I'm going to die!' That's a big drama. It's a real drama—I'm not dismissing it as unreal. We take it as real and must take it as real. If all the time you were watching a film you were thinking, 'this is just a film', you wouldn't get drawn in, you wouldn't be affected. You have to forget it's a film. You have to forget it's not real. It's the same with our lives. We forget about being the One and at a deep level accept the reality of the world, accept being separate, accept being mortal. But then hopefully you re-awaken to being the One. Yet you have been so deeply conditioned to feel separate that you find yourself aware not only of being the One but at the same time continuing to think and feel and act as if you are a separate person. Seeing you are the One doesn't mean you stop experiencing the drama of being a person, the unpredictability of life, your lack of control of others and even of yourself, the feeling of being separate and mortal, but now you have access at the same time to who you really are. This makes all the difference.

Peter: There is fear there.

Richard: Yes, life is a roller-coaster ride. Yes, it's frightening at times. I'm not suggesting it's an easy ride. But I think life is harder if you don't see who you really are. Much harder.

Living from who you are is a life of discovery, a great adventure. In our hearts we want adventure. We don't want to just sit at home doing nothing all day long. At least, I don't! When you see who you are, when you see you have removed your head from the top of your body, so to speak, it's like taking a cork out of a bottle. Now your life can flow. Take the cork out of the bottle by seeing there's no cork! All you need do is look. It's not there. Pop! Champagne! Celebration. Time to party! It's not always easy but it's harder if you keep your head on.

Andrew: Keep on coming back.

Richard: Keep on coming back. And when we have the opportunity to share being the One with friends, like today, it's inspiring and infectious.

Chapter 25

One Awareness

Richard: I hear both my voice and your voice in this One Consciousness, so I am speaking with two voices. Is that also true for you?

Barbara: Yes!

Richard: Now I am the One sharing awareness of being the One with another who is also the One. It's a dream come true. Andrew, you know exactly what it's like to be the One, don't you? You are the One, aren't you? Is everything inside you?

Andrew: Yes.

Richard: Do you see what is happening? We are behaving as if we are separate beings here, yet we are also aware of being one — the One.

Andrew: Yes.

Richard: When we are with others, normally we are acknowledging being separate. All day long I am acknowledging I am Richard. You are acknowledging you are Andrew. When you look at me, I feel you are affirming I am Richard because you are nodding. And I am nodding at you, so you have the feeling I am affirming you are Andrew. But in this room we are now admitting in public that we are not only the one we see in the mirror but we are also the One. When we bring awareness of who we really are onto the front burner, this makes a profound difference in the social situation. It's a new development in society. You are aware now that you are built Open for everybody here.

Anne: Are you saying we are all the same Awareness?

Richard: That is what I am saying!

Anne: That is what I am understanding. We are all the same Awareness.

Richard: Yes. But I don't want you just to try and understand what I am saying, I want you to notice it yourself and express it in your own way. Of course we have to search for the words to begin with because we are not used to articulating this Reality, this two-sided Reality — being both the One and one-amongst-many.

Anne: It's as though your intellect gets in the way of your experience.

Richard: Normally, yes. But now we can use our intellect to celebrate our experience. Our intellect doesn't have to get in the way. Intellect arises within the One. It's an expression of the One.

Chapter 26

Freedom

Richard: Here's something else to notice — this room does not have four complete walls. How many walls can you see?

James: Three.

Richard: The fourth wall is missing. I have a friend who is in prison and this observation is precious to him because it means he's not in prison. We can see we are not in this room. To be in a room you would have to be surrounded by four walls and a floor and a ceiling, but there are only three walls here.

Dale: I'm sitting in a corner so I can see all four!

Richard: Okay! Three walls, or four walls and no corner! But seeing there is a gap somewhere — right where you are — is seeing you are not enclosed, not boxed in. This is not primarily about *feeling* free, it is about *seeing* you are free — seeing the way you are built. You are built free, not enclosed, however you *feel*. You are not contained in this room. My friend in prison sees he is not in prison — prison is in him. Of course he is aware of both sides of himself in the sense that he knows that as well as not being in prison, he *is* in prison and he can't get out. Actually that applies to us all in the sense that we find ourselves in situations we can't get out of. But privately, as who you really are, you are not in that situation, it is in you. Now you can be aware of both sides of yourself. Only having the outside view of yourself is to be imprisoned and that's all there is to it. But to have the Inner View as well is to enjoy your Inner Freedom. Living from this Freedom makes a huge difference in your life.

Roger: Isn't that why they say, 'You are your thoughts?' If you think you are imprisoned then you are.

Richard: Yes. Don't just trust your thoughts, look as well.

Diana: I thought you were not your thoughts?

Richard: I think Roger was meaning that we believe what our thoughts say we are. My thoughts say I am Richard sitting over here. Well, that's true. But it is also true that I am not Richard, I am Space for the world.

Eric: The direct experience of it is so powerful. Our conditioned thoughts and images about ourselves tell us we are deficient or lacking, so *seeing* your Essential Nature is liberating.

Richard: Yes, this Freedom speaks for itself. What a treasure.

Eric: The more you look at it, the more you see.

Richard: Yes, it never runs dry. It gets brighter—it's not a colour, it's not bright or dark, but somehow it gets brighter.

We get lost in our thoughts but fortunately our True Nature is only a look away. You don't have to struggle back up some mountain to get to who you really are. Just look. Now I am seeing it. It is very kind—it is making itself freely and immediately available.

Nigel: I imagine over time we will get less distracted or sucked in by thoughts, so to speak.

Richard: I think this deepens and deepens in so many ways. It's not a recipe for utopia or perfection—perfection is only here at our Centre, not there in the world. But my God, being aware of this makes a difference! You have found the Centre. This is powerful, it's therapeutic. But we need to do it and not just think about it. Today we are supporting each other, helping each other stay awake to who we really are.

Chapter 27

Inner Freedom

Gloria: We were talking about the One and the Many. I'm sitting here and I am the One aware of what is happening. But what about all our neuroses, our patterns and habits, the personality and all of that? How does that relate to the One? How do we get past all of that?

Richard: First, there is a very real sense in which you are what you look like. Everyone is reflecting your appearance back to you and you take it on. The basic message you receive from society is that you are a thing, a person. It's vital to take on that identity so that you can function in society. But being a 'thing' is also a problem because things confront other things. And being a thing also means you will die. It's not surprising, then, believing you are a thing, if you have a few neuroses!

But when you see through the basic assumption that you are a thing and you see you are No-thing, does that mean that your conditioning and your neuroses get all cleared up? Does it mean you no longer have problems? Does it mean you no longer identify with the one-in-the-mirror? Not in my experience. I am still identified with Richard. I still have problems. To be a person is to be complicated, it is to have problems, so when I see who I really am, because I continue being a person, I continue having problems. And yet, Seeing does change something. Now I see that deep down in the foundation of my being I am free. I am not a conditioned thing. I have no restrictions at all. This makes a difference.

This deep sense of freedom you cannot get in any other way. You can get relative freedom from solving this or that problem, but when you sort out one problem another appears. That's life. But when you come Home to who you really are you sort out the basic problem each time you look, the problem of being a limited, mortal thing. This awareness of your deep inner freedom then gradually affects every area of your life.

Chapter 28
Experience and Meaning

You've got the experience of who you really are but your understanding of it is piecemeal. Your understanding will never be complete. If you feel there's something about your True Self that you don't understand, then welcome to the club! No one has a complete understanding of their True Self. If you're thinking that someone else is Seeing but you're not, the reality is that they are simply responding to this basic, neutral experience in a different way from you. You've got the experience—you can't not get it. Their response, their reaction, is simply different from yours, and whatever anyone's reaction, it will pass. Nothing stays forever. If you are feeling confused about who you really are, welcome to the club! In the outward direction everyone's vision is obscure, in the inward direction everyone's is clear. I think we can tolerate the obscurity and our lack of complete understanding in the outward direction because of the Clarity we find in the inward direction. We've got the experience of our True Nature one hundred per cent, whenever we choose to attend to it, and meanwhile our understanding comes and goes. The 'wow' comes and goes.

The experience of who you really are is neutral. The fact it is neutral is valuable because it means there's no hierarchy of seers here. You can't see this better or worse than anyone else. It's a neutral observation of something-happening-in-Nothing. Because it's not dependent on understanding, you can see it at will. You can now, at will, choose to notice that you do not see your own face, instead you see the world. This is not dependent on someone else agreeing. It is not dependent on you thinking about it in a certain way. This means you can notice it anywhere, anytime, even when you're having a bad time. When you are having a bad time you still can't see your face.

We can use the bad times as an excuse—I'm going to wait until the problem goes and then I'm going to notice my True Nature. But you can notice the Space whilst the problem is there. In fact probably the most important moment to notice this is when you are having a hard time. You have no excuse now—you know where to look. Look for your face. It's not an obscure, difficult thing—just look.

Dale: The more I get acquainted with the exercises and just my own practice, it continues to keep deepening. It got to a point where I realised it's impossible to know what this is. We are always trying to put this in a box but when you relax into what you can directly know, this becomes everything. It becomes exciting, a possibility displaying itself—how could you be bored? It just keeps deepening.

Chapter 29

Let's Dance

I watched an interview on television with the Englishwoman Jane Goodall. In the 1960s when she was a teenager she worked in Africa with Louis Leaky, the paleo-anthropologist. He was trying to find the bones that would link chimpanzees and apes with humans—the 'missing link'. Jane Goodall's job was to study the behaviour of chimpanzees to see if any of their behaviour was similar to human behaviour. If she could observe such similarities in behaviour, then this would support Leaky's idea that back in pre-history there existed an ancestor that we humans and apes have in common, in whom such behaviour originated.

For example, in this interview she described walking down a path with a chimp—as you do!—and they stopped for a rest. She had a piece of fruit in her pocket and she offered it to the chimp. The chimp took the fruit but then for a moment held Jane's hand, looked her in the eye, then squeezed her hand—and dropped the fruit. Jane interpreted this behaviour as—'Thank you very much. I don't want the fruit but I don't want to hurt your feelings by not taking it.' That is something a person might do. 'I don't want it, but thanks.' Then you squeeze the person's hand to indicate you don't want to hurt their feelings.

Anyway she observed that each evening the chimpanzees she was studying used to go to a waterfall. They didn't go there to eat or drink or sleep. They just went and looked at the waterfall. As they were looking at it they did a little dance—as Jane Goodall interpreted it. They moved from foot to foot as they were looking at the waterfall. The way she understood it was that they were noticing something extraordinary—the fact that the water was always coming in, always going out, yet was always there. She had the feeling that the chimps couldn't understand how this could be. How could the water always be coming in, always be going out, yet always be there? Very mysterious! So in the face of this mystery, as a response to this mystery and miracle, the chimpanzees danced.

So I say, look out from the Void and there is this miracle of life. This present moment is always coming in, it's always going out, yet it's always there. For me the appropriate response to this mystery is not to write a doctoral thesis but it is to dance. The life that arises here in the Void is a mystery, a miracle, a gift. This waterfall of the present moment is pouring in who knows from where? It's pouring out—who knows where it's going? Yet it is always there. Always there. Inexplicable, a gift, a miracle.

Anne: The dance of life.

Richard: Yes.

Anne: Your optimism gives us all a lot.

Richard: I'm optimistic because the impossible has happened, is happening—Being. After that, what is not possible? The impossible has happened—is happening now!

Chapter 30

Pain and Resistance

Before the workshop began this gentleman was asking about whether or not seeing who you really are helps with pain. Hold out your hand and look at it. You see colour and shape there but here at your Centre you see no colour or shape—you are empty for your hand. Now make a fist so your hand becomes tense. Does the Space get tense? No. Now relax. Your body tenses and then relaxes but the Space isn't affected. Now gently press your thumbnail into one of your fingers so you feel some slight discomfort. Is the Space hurt? No. Though you are aware the Space is not affected, do you still feel the discomfort? Yes. But the discomfort is not central. Does being aware of this make a difference to how you cope with tension and pain? I say yes, but find out for yourself!

Say you've got a problem and you don't know how to solve it. Hold the problem in your mind, in this wise Space. I'm sure the Source will come up with some kind of answer—though it might not be the answer you expect or want! It's a very wise Space, self-evidently, because it is. It knows how to Be.

Here's another experiment. Look at your hands and notice you're looking at them from No-thing, from Emptiness. The Emptiness receives the colour of your hands. It doesn't interfere with the colour, does it? It's just Empty, it's just Open for the colour. It doesn't say 'No' to the colour. Now put your palms together and press them one against the other with equal pressure on both sides. They don't move. You can feel them resisting each other. The Space accepts the resistance, doesn't it? Now stop. Now push with the right hand and let the left hand yield. Does the Space prefer yielding to pushing, or winning to losing? No. It says yes to everything.

On the surface, speaking as Richard, sometimes I resist things and sometimes I accept them. Sometimes I resist pain and some-times I accept it—eventually, when I have to! But deep down, as my True Self , I always accept what is happening, including pain.

Deep down I say yes to everything.

Does it make a difference to see that deep down you're always saying yes, that you're always welcoming the present moment? It does. Seeing who you really are is a profound yes to life, and accepting and welcoming life is different from resisting it. But test this. See who you are and see how things work out when deep down you are welcoming life, even though on the surface you might be resisting what's happening.

Ian: I have some pretty strong noes in me.

Richard: Yes, me too.

Ian: So I can't agree that I say yes to everything. Even at a deep level I have a sense that certain things are right, certain things are wrong.

Richard: But does the Space resist anything?

Ian: I don't know.

Richard: Well, check it out. I find it doesn't.

Ian: Yes, but if you had a fist coming at your nose you'd get out of the way, right?

Richard: Yes. But I'm distinguishing between me as Richard and me as who I really am. As I said, Richard resists. Hopefully he gets out of the way of an inbound fist! But who I really am...

Margaret: ...says yes to getting out of the way.

Richard: Exactly. It's appropriate to say yes to some things and no to other things. Things resist things. That's what things do. Things resist things but No-thing doesn't resist anything. Now, are you a thing at Centre or are you No-thing? Only you can say. If you're No-thing you're not resisting anything. But have a look. Look now. What do you find there? Right where I am I find No-thing—nothing but Space for the world.

This unconditional Openness isn't an attitude. It's not a feeling. It's not an achievement. You can't do it more or less. It's not a matter of degree, is it? You can't be a little bit Empty. But downstream from the Source you can be a bit surrendered or a lot surrendered. For certain things it's very good to be surrendered but for other things it's not. So downstream there's always a rhythm between yes and no, between surrender and resistance. But here in the Source, upstream of all things, you are always built Open—face *there* to No-face *here*.

These experiments are ways of moving our attention very simply from *there* to *here*. You see how simple it is. How absolutely available it is. How you can't do it wrong. The only time you can see who you are is now. Seeing this doesn't need confirmation from anybody else. It's so practical. And loving. It goes deeper and deeper and deeper. This way, in the view in, it never changes but that way, in the view out, it goes deeper and deeper. It's a matter of bringing your attention to it. I suppose you could say that the more you do it, the more it becomes your default position.

David: What about fear, like in the story when God comes into Being and then decides to forget, when he risks not remembering he's God? I sense that fear of not remembering, of completely losing the Self. What do you suggest when that fear comes up?

Richard: Right now are you seeing who you are? Yes. That's all you can do. You cannot guarantee the future. You can only see who you really are *now*. There's great freedom in that. You can't fix or capture the Space. Anyway that fear is part of the game, isn't it? It's in the game, *there*. You are free of it *here* where you are. You can see that now. You are absolutely free of that fear now even while you're feeling it. It's like pain—you feel it *there* and not *here*. So this is not a promise that you'll never feel afraid again or you won't feel depressed or you won't feel hurt. But it's a promise that you can always see who you really are here and now, which is seeing that there's no fear or depression or pain right where you are. And paradoxically, seeing it now is seeing it forever because the seeing itself is out of time.

Of course, don't believe what I'm saying, test it for yourself.

Joan: Perhaps another way of interpreting that story is that we are in the process of remembering that we are God, or the Vastness, or the Absolute.

Richard: A good way of putting it. The fact that this experience is so obvious and available to us all means there's nothing to argue about. Everyone has a valid view from the Source and everyone's expression of this is valid. Seeing we are the One at centre empowers individuality and uniqueness.

Chapter 31
Fear of Losing Self

Dale: Sometimes people feel disorientated and even frightened when they first come to this. Can you share about that from your experience?

Richard: I think we can all probably understand how it could be like that because this is such a different way of experiencing yourself compared to the social view of you. It can be scary for people to point back at themselves and see nothing there — suddenly you feel you've disappeared, that you don't exist. This can feel strange and uncomfortable, or even frightening. Perhaps you are tempted to run away from it.

But if you don't run, if you continue attending, continue seeing who you are, you see that even though you are 'nothing', you still are. Being is indestructible. And then you see that even though you are seeing you are 'nothing', that you are Being, the social view of you continues. Your self-consciousness remains. Instead of losing your social self, you realise your social self is simply not central — the Space is central, Being is central. So you haven't really lost your self — rather you have *placed* it, located it out there where it belongs.

As you experiment with noticing this, as you take the Seeing for a ride as it were, you find that it's safe. In fact, it's a brilliant arrangement — privately you are Space, publicly you are a person. Now you live both sides of your identity and you find this works, and works better than just being the one-in-the-mirror.

Let me add that I have found it valuable to have friends who See because if you feel disoriented by Seeing, and there have been times when I have felt disoriented, others who are Seeing will probably understand. And hopefully they will help you understand that a little bit of disorientation is normal. If you didn't feel a bit disoriented at some point, it would be rather odd, wouldn't it? You have spent years identifying with the one-in-the-mirror and now you see that from your point of view you are Space for the world. That's a radical shift. Hopefully it *will* upset you!

Awareness of who you really are goes together with awareness of being an individual. It doesn't cancel out or dissolve your individuality. Rather it places it. So although you are now seeing you are boundless, at the same time you are aware of your personal boundaries. I see that I am you, but even so I'm not going to give you my wallet! As a person I understand well enough where I end and you begin. At the same time I see that I am you, that all the world is mine and I am infinitely rich, so maybe I will give you my wallet after all! There isn't a fixed rule here.

Chapter 32

Problem-free

Ian: I'm aware of a struggle internally. On the one hand I notice this effort inside me, this belief that I have to create this experience of one Consciousness. I notice my brain thinking I have to create this Reality. On the other hand I'm learning that I don't have to keep creating this, I don't have to keep trying to create the experience, because the experience is already happening.

Richard: Seeing who you really are doesn't mean you don't have these kinds of feelings — the feeling, for example, that you should make the Seeing happen. That reaction goes on in the Space. You are not doing it wrong. It would be hard if Seeing meant that we shouldn't have those kinds of reactions because we've been taught every day that to get on in life we have to do this, that and the other. So those kinds of thoughts and feelings are deeply embedded in us. And that's okay.

Ian: It's happening in the Space.

Richard: Yes, it is.

Ian: Just hanging there.

Richard: Yes, just hanging there. Magic. As the One I'm creating a problem now, arising in the Nothing! If you had no problems after seeing who you are, in about five minutes you would pray for them because problems mean challenges — which involve going on adventures and discovering new things. Yes, it's sometimes difficult, and sometimes it's very difficult, but it's a learning process. Anyway you will get problems whether you want them or not!

Ian: The experience I am having now is that they are just in the Space.

Thomas: Douglas Harding said that if you have a problem, imagine it in your hand and hold it there. The problem is there.

Richard: Hold your hand out and imagine you are holding your problem. Think of a problem you've got in your life now. A real problem you've got and imagine it in your hand. The problem is there. Now notice your arm comes back to the Open Space. Your arm comes out of Nothing, out of the Single Eye. Problem there, no problem here!

Chapter 33

Trust

Alex: The one-in-the-mirror, the little one—is there ever any real change aside from the developmental stages? Do you find that awareness of who you really are influences the little one?

Richard: Yes, more and more, deeper and deeper. I think it happens differently for everyone though there are general themes. As the reality of who I really am gradually sinks in, my respect for the One grows. Therefore I am inclined to hand over to that One more and more, to trust it more and more. This is never a complete thing in my experience, it's a rhythm—sometimes I resist. So there's a dialogue, a rhythm between resistance and surrender, between doubt and trust. The more I go on, the more I see who is here, the more I think, 'You are smart! You seem to know what you are doing!' You—meaning the One.

Alex: I laugh because we did the experiment where you push one hand against the other and you asked, 'Does the Space have a preference?' It's so clear that it doesn't. Then two seconds later I can have a conversation and completely forget I had that understanding!

Richard: Yes, we're all a bit worried about you, Alex!

Jennifer: I don't know what you mean by 'trust it'. Trust it to do what?

Richard: Well, to take care of you.

Brian: It has never changed, so of course you can trust something that has never changed.

Richard: Yes, you can trust it always to be there. But how can you be sure it's going to take care of you? I can't be sure, but now I do have the choice of trusting it or not. I certainly don't trust it all the time. Sometimes I doubt that it is taking care of me. But this means that now I'm on an interesting journey, an adventure. I'm aware of the One and aware of the possibility of trusting it. I find that the more I do trust it, the more trustworthy I realise it is. It's mysterious how it functions. It is supremely wise, and loving.

Chapter 34

Remembering

Diana: It's a wonderful sensation to have awareness of this Nothingness here. It feels very light. But how do you not forget about that Awareness when you are out in the world? How can you remember the awareness of your Nothingness all the time?

Richard: There are different answers to this question. Here are a few ideas. These experiments are brilliant, simple, practical reminders that you can use in your everyday life. Seeing who you really are is not an esoteric, abstract idea. When you are with another person you can notice that it's face there to Space here—you are built Open for them. When you look at me now you only see Richard's face, you don't see your own—face-to-No-face. You can see that. Whenever you are with anyone you can notice that. It's practical. It's non-verbal, so you don't have to say anything or even think anything. A person in a shop, your beloved, anyone, it's always the same—face there to No-face here. Or you can notice your Single Eye—it doesn't matter if anyone else is there or not, or where you are. You could even point, perhaps when you are alone somewhere. Point now at your No-face. There you are. You can't see your face. Or when you are driving, see that you are Still whilst the scenery moves. When you close your eyes in bed, see that you have no boundary. So these are practical tips and reminders that you can use anywhere, at any time. That's one idea. Though probably the most important thing is that you want to be aware of who you really are. Then you will find your way to that, one way or another.

Growing up in society is becoming aware of yourself as a person in the eyes of others. You take on that identity. I am seeing myself through your eyes as Richard. I can't see Richard but I am taking that identity from you like I take the image from the mirror. So I am acting *as if* Richard is here. A baby hasn't learned to do that yet. But because everybody is self-conscious in the society where the baby is growing up, the baby learns to be self-conscious. It's infectious. You can't avoid it. You can't ignore, deny or reject your personal identity, otherwise you couldn't function in society. In other words, being a person is a socially infectious thing and it continues to be so until the day you die. One way or another you are continually being reminded by others of your personal identity, and you are reminding others of theirs.

Yet I am also aware that I am the One. Here in this workshop we are in a mini-society where awareness of our True Self is on the front burner. This is also infectious, especially when we communicate about it. Then, as well as affirming and confirming each other's social identity, we are also affirming and confirming our True Identity. It's a powerful thing to declare who you really are in public, to communicate about our One Self. 'I am the One! Are you One? Yes? Brilliant!' When we bring awareness of our True Self into consciousness, into the social situation, as we are doing today, it is as infectious as awareness of our public identity. Communicating with others about who we really are raises awareness of our True Self for everyone. That's why I encourage people to use their voices. In this way we are helping each other be aware of being the One. Though this Reality needs no outside confirmation, we are confirming it.

The more people there are who say yes to this Reality, the more the social atmosphere changes in the direction of facilitating and supporting this Awareness. This is the 'work' that has to be done—living from and sharing who we really are, though it's more like play than work. Here in this workshop today we are keeping this awareness on the front burner—helping one another remain awake to our True Self. Actually, now that you have met these others here who are seeing who they are, you don't have to meet them ever again and you will always be in touch with them—because there is only One. When you are seeing who you are, you are seeing as and for everyone. So at a deep level we are supporting each other when we See, even when we are not in each other's company.

But as well as that comforting fact, these days there are many opportunities to be with others who see who they are, either in actual company or online or in some other way. There's a growing community around the world that is saying yes to this Reality. That's a powerful support group, as it were. That's why I am here in this workshop—to support and be supported, to remind and be reminded of who I really am, to enjoy hearing our many voices in this one Silence. So having friends that you share this Seeing with can really help you stay awake to the Seeing.

Diana: What happens eventually? Let's say if I do see who I am all the time, constantly, will there be some kind of transformation?

Richard: Once you see who you are, is there a sudden and total shift? Are you then always Seeing so that you never go back to the old way of being? Well, Being is always here. When you see who you really are you see that your True Self is always here. It has never not been here. So in a sense nothing changes, except you notice that which never changes. Of course I haven't always been thinking about who I really am or saying yes to it at a conscious level, but it is always here. So what changes is not the view in to the Space but our responses and reactions to the Space, which are in our view out. Appreciating or thinking about the Space are reactions—you might suddenly have the thought, the realisation, that you are the One. Then you hope that you will always feel this, always realise this, but you won't. It's a thought, or a feeling, so it fades away.

Diana: That's what I was talking about. I want to feel it for the rest of my life.

Richard: I know. But you won't. Any feelings you have about the One will pass. You know, it's actually a blessing that even the deepest realisation about being the One goes because if you were saddled with it, it would become a burden. Anyway, when a deep, precious realisation goes, then it makes room for something new. In time, something even deeper and more meaningful will arise out of the One. If you were able to hold onto a realisation it would only block something even better from arising, something that is waiting for you there in the Mystery!

Chapter 35
The Joy without a Shadow

Richard: When you shine a light on anything, it casts a shadow. I can see the shadow of John's shoes there. Shine a light on me and my shadow will be on the wall behind me. Everything has a shadow. We can also say that every joy has a shadow. Every good thing ends. Even if it doesn't end badly, it will end, so in that sense it has a shadow. Something might be so good that you want it to last forever but it doesn't. There's the shadow. There's the dissatisfaction in life, the suffering. I think that's what the Buddha was talking about when he said that life is suffering, life is unsatisfactory. Everything ends, everything collapses, every individual thing finally falls apart, every loved one dies. You as a person will die. This is reality. I think that seeing who you really are brings you up to speed with reality. Everything has a shadow. It's understandable if at some point you feel depressed because everything passes. I think that if you haven't ever experienced a kind of underlying depression and sadness then perhaps you haven't really acknowledged that everything passes, that everyone dies. This is reality. If you love life, if you love someone, how can you not feel sad at some point, knowing that that person will die? All that you hold dear will turn to dust.

But we don't have to stop with this realisation. Go deeper and look underneath that depression and sadness, underneath everything that comes and goes and you find that who you really are does not come or go. In fact, in a sense physically as well as psychologically, your True Self casts no shadow. What I mean is that if you shine a light on any individual thing in this room, it will cast a shadow on the background behind it. But now look at the Whole View. You are shining the light of awareness on it but the Whole View has no background, so there's nowhere for a shadow to fall. This is the one 'thing' that has no shadow because it has no background—the Whole has no background. And whereas every individual thing comes and goes, underneath all these temporary things is Being which does not come or go. Now you have found the joy that casts no shadow. Now you can choose to welcome this truth, this Joy, into your life.

People who say, 'I'm realistic, life sucks', have not gone deep enough. Of course, every individual thing comes and goes, so in that sense life sucks. But if you go deeper you will find the place that does not suck, that does not come or go. Now live consciously as the Unchanging One, the Unborn and the Undying Light. You will find that this Light then floods back up through all these joys that do cast shadows and infuses them with a different feel. You are no longer looking for the joy that casts no shadow out there in the things that come and go because you have found it where it is, at your Centre. You have discovered that which does not end. So now you can appreciate the things that do come and go and know that they will end without their end being catastrophic.

Roger: It's beautiful when you allow all the shadow stuff to come up, all the stuff we reject, and see that underneath it is the divine.

Richard: You can have compassion for yourself and others. I slipped up, but what did I expect? Life slipped up, what did I expect? But Being doesn't slip up. Being is the supreme success story.

Chapter 36
Feeling for Others

Kevin: When you say 'No' to someone, it doesn't matter what their reaction is. It doesn't affect who you really are.

Richard: Yes, their reaction doesn't affect the Space. This is important and true. But I find that Seeing doesn't mean I feel detached from others. I feel profoundly involved with others. Of course it's different for everyone. But when you see who you are, you see there's no barrier between you and others. They are right here in you. Your face now is mine. If you look sad, in a way your sadness is my own.

When we are unaware of being faceless and Open, it's common to feel uncomfortable when someone looks at us. We feel self-conscious. In turn we tend to avoid looking at others. We don't want to cause them discomfort, and we don't want them to catch us looking at them—at least for more than about a second! So we end up hardly ever looking steadily, attentively, at anyone. They say there are two situations where someone might look steadily at someone else—either when they have fallen in love with them or when they are going to kill them! Otherwise, it's taboo. If this is the case, how can we really know someone? I was once working in a counselling centre and mentioned to another counsellor that one of the experiments in our workshops involves looking at someone and noticing we are Space for them. The counsellor looked horrified. "I never even look at my husband, never mind a stranger," she replied.

But when you see you are faceless, you re-awaken the innocence and openness of the child in you, and you begin to look at people without so much self-consciousness or fear. That's my experience anyway. Perhaps you are less pre-occupied with what people think of you when you're out of the way, when you're occupied with them rather than yourself. You find yourself looking, taking in that person in a non-intrusive way. I think Sherlock Holmes said, 'If you want to find something, there's nothing like looking!' Well, if you want to know others, there's nothing like looking!

So I don't think seeing who you really are lets you off the hook of being involved with and feeling for others. In fact perhaps one reason why people resist Seeing, if they do, is because their intuition tells them it would mean a much deeper letting in of others, and with that a deeper experience of the suffering of the world. Rather than being a way of distancing yourself from others, Seeing is an ever deepening involvement with others. Although nothing can hurt you as the One, at the same time, living as the One you become more vulnerable.

Kevin: That's powerful.

Laura: It is loving either through identity or loving through the One. Loving your children through an identity or loving your children through the One—it's a different thing.

Richard: That's beautiful.

Angela: Do you find that you naturally flow between those identifications?

Richard: Yes. Not only can I not get rid of my human self, I don't want to. It is precious. If you want to get rid of your human self, what does that say about your attitude to others? Why bother with them?

Angela: Yes, why bother with them?

Richard: Why bother with them? You are deeply, deeply connected and identified with your human self. It is very special and you need it. The One needs it. Because we have learned to identify with our human self and take responsibility for that person and have some limited understanding of what it is to be a person, we can appreciate what other people are going through in their lives. If you don't go through that process of identification you can't empathise. When you wake up to the One your empathy deepens because now you are not only recognising that others feel like you do though you don't experience their feelings directly, and they think like you do though you never experience their thoughts, and so on—now you also recognise that they are looking out of the One, just like you are. This is an even deeper empathy, isn't it? You know exactly what it is like to be who they really are because that is what you are too.

Chapter 37

Owning the Wor~

William: There was a time in my life when I w
the things I didn't have. I only had a little of what   ~ave.
Now I have everything. When I visit Dale's house i   ~y house too!

Dale: How about paying the mortgage!

William: I have a unique type of ownership! I own your house
from here and I don't pay the mortgage! No matter where I go, if I
am on an airplane it's my airplane. All the people on it are keeping
me company. It's like being in a movie. I cast everybody to play
those roles in my movie so we can have this story unfold.

Richard: One time when I was travelling with Douglas Harding we pulled off the motorway into a cafe and had a cup of
tea. Douglas started talking about the cafe emerging magically
out of Nothing. There it was with all the staff ready to serve us
and everything up and running. You pay a couple of pounds for
a coffee and look what you get for the money! A fully function-
ing cafe. You are Space for it, so it's yours. But you don't have to
worry about maintaining it. As soon as you have finished your
coffee you put the cafe back in the Void. You fold it up and put it
away. When you need it, you take it out of the Void. When you
no longer need it, you put it back!

Peter: We can create anything.

Richard: The Void can. The One can. Incredible. It's so playful,
so creative, so appreciative, so rich, so fun-loving.

You are always at Home. I haven't gone anywhere — Dale and
all of you have arrived in me. You are my guests here in my Home.
Then in a short while you will disappear back into the Void and
London will arrive in me, and London will be my guest in my
Home here. This is true for us all. This engenders a different
feeling about life, doesn't it? You are at Home wherever you are.
That's the truth, so let's get used to it!

Peter: Life is visiting you.

d: Yes. It's amazing, a miracle, a gift. Incredible. Where ou come from?

Peter: Flowing through you.

Chapter 38

Coming Home

Margaret: Typically we are not aware of the Space, of looking in this inward direction. Typically we are looking in the outward direction. So now are we expanding our perspective to include both directions?

Richard: Yes. The baby is just looking out, it is not looking back at itself yet. Growing up is learning to look back at yourself from the point of view of others. But we stop half-way at our human appearance. I am imagining how I appear through your eyes—in a way I'm looking back at myself. I'm imagining what I look like from your point of view. I imagine Richard here. When I see who I really am I come all the way home and look all the way back to the Centre where there is Nothing. I had the right direction before but I was stopping at my face. Now I am coming all the way home to my No-face. Of course in the end there isn't a here or a there. These terms are provisional. It's both together somehow. But because we've got this idea of here and there, now we can say that we come all the way here, all the way Home.

Point in again. Now point out at the same time—two-way pointing. It's a gesture. We are under the delusion that there is something here at our Centre, so now we dispel that delusion by looking. We are under the delusion that we are looking out of a thing here. We look to see if that's true.

Margaret: I just got this! I think what you were saying is true—we stop at our reflection, at our face. We stop there. I don't think I ever really recognised that. You don't have to stop there, you keep going.

Richard: Yes, all the way Home.

Chapter 39

Two Languages

Richard: When you see who you really are, in a way you learn to speak a new language. Before you see who you really are, the word 'I' means you as a person. But when you wake up to who you really are you realise that 'I' can also mean you as the One. Do you now have to swap one vocabulary for the other? Do you have to get rid of the first meaning of the word that refers to you as a person now that you are aware of your True Self? No. Now you speak two languages. Which language you speak depends on who you are talking to. When you are talking to someone who knows nothing about their True Self you don't use the word 'I' as meaning the One, you use it for yourself as a person. So in that situation I use the word 'I' as referring to Richard. But when I'm speaking with someone who does see who they really are, then I can switch back and forth between both meanings. Kids who grow up with a French and an English parent might start a sentence in French and end it in English. You move back-and-forth easily between the two languages. It's the same with this. You can be flexible. This is richer and more intelligent than thinking you have to stick to one language. I say that I'm going to get into my car and watch the scenery move through my Stillness. There you go — I started the sentence as Richard moving and ended it as the One who never moves. Why not? If the person you are talking to sees who they are, they understand.

Kevin: The idea of being the One is not part of our language. Our language has not caught up. It's catching up now.

Richard: Yes, we are learning a new language.

Kevin: I hear some people referring to themselves as 'this organism' rather than say, 'Johnny...'

Richard: When you realise that the experience is non-verbal your emphasis is not on getting it exactly right in language. If you do try and get it exactly right you'll become like a lawyer. 'There is anger arising.' That way of speaking seems clumsy to me. You mean you're angry?

Chapter 40

Unconditional Openness

Richard: If I drop out of the Face Game but you still want to play, I don't mind now, really. If you are playing the Face Game it doesn't mean I have to play. And my not playing is not something I do separately from you—I'm seeing who I am as you and for you. I am not Seeing separately from you.

Seeing who you are is non-intrusive, it's not imposing anything. It's letting people be as they are and it's receiving who they are being. The Space is unconditionally Open. It doesn't say, 'I'm going to be Open for you as long as you behave yourself, as long as you don't play the Face Game.' No. I'd like you to behave yourself, I'd like you to be aware of who you really are, but if you don't do what I want you to do, I am still you. In fact, not playing the Face Game is a private thing. It doesn't depend on others not playing. In a sense it has nothing to do with others. You just look for yourself and that's it.

Most people don't know of any other way of being apart from playing the Face Game. But when people see who they are, other people feel it. It's a loving thing to do. People think, 'I would like some of that.' When you are conscious of your Openness you are communicating that Openness—in your own way you will be transmitting that Openness.

Being who you really are is sane, it's healthy. When you are Seeing, naturally you have compassion for others who are playing the Face Game because they are unaware of this treasure within themselves. You're not there judging them—'You're playing the Face Game and I'm not.' It's not 'us and them' any more. You are embracing everyone as yourself.

Chapter 41
Independent of Feeling

Raise your hands and explore the edge of your Single Eye. All the way round your hands disappear into this vast Openness, Silence, Stillness. It's non-verbal and non-emotional. This experience is not dependent on whether you are feeling good or bad. You are simply noticing you cannot see your head. It's just a fact, an observation. This neutrality is a great advantage. Seeing your True Self is not dependent on your mood. It's just there, whatever you are feeling—you don't see your head.

This experience may or may not mean something to you. Someone in the circle might have a strong, positive reaction to seeing they are headless. 'Wow, that's amazing!' Meanwhile someone else is thinking, 'James seems to have got it but I'm not feeling like he's feeling, so I can't have got it.' No! You've got it but you're having a different reaction, that's all. We distinguish between the non-verbal, neutral experience—you can't see your head, you can't see anything here—and your reaction to it. Everyone's reaction to it is going to be different. So I'm affirming the validity of your reaction, whatever it is. Even if it's 'So what?' That's a valid reaction, isn't it? Of course. But you still can't see your head. Even if it means nothing to you, you can't avoid the experience! True?

Mark: Yes.

Richard: Are you having a 'wow' experience?

Mark: Not quite, but certainly feeling a little dizzy!

Chapter 42

Sharing with Children

James: What about sharing awareness of who we really are with young children?

Richard: We are all coming from this Space but babies and infants are coming from here without the complication of feeling self-conscious. In this regard they are our teachers. We are not teaching them about being Capacity, we are teaching them to join the human club! That's our job. We are not teaching them to be who they really are—if anything, they are teaching us that! So I wouldn't bring up the subject of being the One with a child. A child is in the business of joining the human club, of learning to play the Face Game. Of course if they ask about this kind of thing or they say, 'Mummy, why don't I have a head?' as sometimes happens, since you know what they mean you can answer their question in a sympathetic, supportive way. In an understanding way. You don't invalidate their experience. If you didn't know about being headless then you might dismiss their experience—'Don't be silly.' But since you do see this you can say, 'I know what you mean, I can't see my head either.'

James: What about teenagers?

Richard: I was a teenager when I came across this, so some teenagers are interested in who they really are. So there's no rule. But basically teenagers are in the business of finding out who they are in the world. The last thing you want to be when you're a teenager is nobody—you want to be somebody. That's totally appropriate. I have a friend whose mother was a member of a spiritual group, a 'non-dual', Advaita group. Her mother didn't like to use the word 'I' because the group's philosophy was that there wasn't an 'I'. So for example, instead of saying you were angry you had to say, 'Anger is arising.' Anyway her mother, thinking she was doing the best thing, wouldn't use the word 'I' with her daughter. Can you imagine how confusing that was? My friend says that when she came across headlessness it really helped her because it enabled her to accept the reality of herself as a person as well as the reality of herself as the One. It was okay to think of herself as a person and use the word 'I'. If we tell our children there isn't an 'I', a self, that really 'we don't exist', we are storing up problems for them. It's obvious, isn't it?

Of course, if a teenager asks you about this, like I asked when I was a teenager, and you know about who you really are, then you are in a great position to respond positively. If anyone asks me about this, whatever their age, I will respond. But as soon as I get the feeling that they don't want to hear any more, I back off. A child, an adult, a teenager, it doesn't matter. It's unproductive and it's not respectful to press this on others. But when someone comes to ask you about this, you can take your foot off the brake and share your experience with them.

Chapter 43
A Curse becomes a Blessing

I directly experience the One, I hear about the Many. It's clear to me that I can't prove there are others. I don't know for certain that you are thinking and feeling and so on. I don't know for certain that you still exist when I can't see you. I used to think that the truth, therefore, is that you don't exist when I can't see you and there is no other consciousness apart from mine—there is no other view out from the One apart from my View. I Alone Am. There is only here and there is only now. So I thought, 'Since that must be the truth then I've really got to live that. There is no one out there so I've got to stop fantasising that there is. Stop it, Richard!' But part of my desire to live free of the delusion of others was not simply a desire to live the truth. I also hoped that if I got rid of the idea of others, then that would solve all my problems—because others were the problem. I thought, 'This seems like a good way forward—look at others without any feeling that there is anyone there, or indeed anyone here. Then all my self-consciousness will go and all my problems with it. No self, no others, no problems.' I tried this but I couldn't do it. I failed. I couldn't get rid of the idea of others or the idea of myself. The feeling of the reality of others persisted. My self-consciousness persisted.

I realised that although I could see there were no others and accepted this to be true, I was acting *as if* there were others, and I couldn't stop doing that. I was acting as if you were there and I was here. I was acting as if there was a 'we'. I couldn't prove there was a 'we' but I couldn't stop acting as if it was true and real. Then I thought, 'The problem here is not the idea of the 'we', the problem is my resistance to it. What happens if I just acknowledge defeat and admit I can't stop acting in this way? I have been so deeply conditioned into this way of being that I can't stop it. I cannot stop acting as if I am real, other people are real, other places are real, other times are real. Instead of resisting it, let me accept it.'

At the same time I began examining more closely my experience of self-consciousness. Looking back in my life it was clear I had always been the Space but I had not always been Richard — as a baby, from my point of view neither myself nor others yet existed. As I moved into infancy and childhood, Richard and others emerged in Consciousness. They became increasingly real. Or I could say — since I am the Source — they emerged out of my own Being. I as the One gave birth to myself and others. I divided into many.

Kierkegaard observed that life is lived forwards and understood backwards. I realised this was true. Looking back at my life I could see meaning in experiences that had little or no meaning for me at the time. Distance lends perspective, it helps make sense of things. But now I realised I could look back not just at my personal development, the changes I had gone through as Richard, and try and make sense of those — I could also look back at the way I as the One had developed, in particular at the fact that I started out as One and then divided into many. Just as I might look back at my personal life and question why I did something, trying to understand my unconscious motives, my hidden intentions that only now were revealing themselves in my actions — now that I could finally see where things had led — now I began looking back as the One and asking myself, 'Why did I as the One divide into many? What were my unconscious intentions, my hidden motives? What was I hoping to achieve by forgetting I was the One and instead becoming one-amongst-many? Why did I do this when the presence of 'self' and 'others' has proved to be so problematic? Why didn't I simply remain in my original state of Oneness, of Aloneness, and avoid all that stress?'

An answer came to me, framed in a kind of story, a myth about the One becoming many. I spoke about it earlier in the workshop. As the One I appeared out of nothing. I happened. Wonder of wonders! Having miraculously achieved Being I wanted to share the wonder and joy I felt about creating myself, but there was no one to share my feelings with — I alone had appeared out of nothing. So, having achieved the impossible feat of creating myself out of nothing, I then did a second astonishing thing — I created others so that I would have someone to talk to! This invention involved a period of forgetting I was the One and becoming a person—the stage of adulthood. This was when I became profoundly convinced of the reality of myself as a person and the reality of others and had no idea I was the One.

Now, in the fourth stage of the seer, I am still identified profoundly with Richard and I'm still very much aware of 'others'. But now I also see who I really am. There are also 'others' in my life who also see who they really are. Which means my original dream has come true. I have achieved what I set out to achieve—I am with others with whom I can share my joy—our joy—about Being. How did the One think up this solution to its problem of loneliness? It's pure genius. But I guess it didn't know what it was doing at the time and only now, through us, is it beginning to see and appreciate what it did!

A thing welcomed is different from a thing resisted. In a sense nothing has changed. I am as identified with Richard as ever and convinced of the reality of others as ever. With this sense of separation comes suffering. What I would give if only I could go back to the eternal peace and quiet of being the Alone without others! Well, I would give nothing at all! I don't want to go back. That's exactly what I wanted to get away from! Now I realise that the point of 'growing up', of going through that painful experience of becoming a person, was to prepare the ground for the next stage of the seer. I began as the One without others. I then forgot about being the Alone and became one-amongst-many. Fortunately I kept going and, rediscovering the One, transformed into the One-that-is-also-many. My dream was to have company. My dream was to be able to share the wonder and joy I feel about Being. My dream has come true—all day today I have been celebrating with you the miracle of who we really are.

How very clever the One is! What I had viewed as a problem—feeling separate—turned out to be one of the very great inventions of the One. Recognising this, my resistance to feeling separate is melting. I begin to accept, and then positively welcome, the experience of being separate. The curse of 'self' and 'others' is tranforming into the blessing of 'self' and 'others'.

Chapter 44

The End

It's the end of the workshop! It's been great to be you all! It's been wonderful to have Seeing on the front burner all day long, and a delight to share our different responses to this Miracle that we are. I hope to see and be you again soon.

Now I am going to put you back into the Void!